Wur bist ’ee gwa-in Siree?

Wur bist 'ee gwa-in Siree?

A History of Stanton Lacy Parish

by

Cliff Smout

Flemish Publications

FLEMISH PUBLICATIONS
Rock Cottage, The Bullring,
Upper Hayton, Ludlow, Shropshire SY8 2AX

First published by Flemish Publications 1998

ISBN 09 533860 07

Set in Times by Logaston Press
and printed in Great Britain by
Antony Rowe, Chippenham, Wilts

Cover illustration: The author's great grandfather, Francis Smout, at Rock Cottage in 1900

To my wife,
Hazel

Contents

Acknowledgements

I wish to thank those people who supplied the documents without which the following book would not have been written, especially the Local Studies Library in Shrewsbury. I also express my thanks to those people in and around the Parish who have tolerated my prying and questions.

Foreword

Stanton Lacy Parish consists of two distinct areas much like the County of Shropshire: one part being flat, while the rest consists of hills and small valleys. These valleys are still known by their Saxon names as 'Hopes', while parishes adjoining to the west have taken the Old English names for their narrow valleys 'Batch' or 'Bach'. Further west on the Welsh border the Welsh name 'Cwm' has been adopted. The lowlands of the parish are the most fertile, with the River Corve running along the broad valley, while the uplands are not so well watered. Witchcot Brook, Studley Gutter, Hope Brook and the Lydehole Brook, which runs down the parish boundary,being the main watercourses.

The parish slopes gently westward to an altitude of 130 metres at Vernolds Common, rising more steeply to the east up to the 262 metre mark at its highest point near Bent Coppices (OS 522803). The soils are mainly clay with freestone subsoil, and limestone ridges in many places. Much of the parish is of outstanding beauty, there being fine views from many points.

The parish has five main areas that are populated: Stanton Lacy village, Vernolds Common, The Hope, Lower and Upper Hayton and Downton, whilst a few cottages and isolated farms dot the remaining area.

There were once two schools but both have now closed. The few children are transported to the Corvedale School at Diddlebury. The Methodist movement once had four chapels, but none remain in use. There are no shops, pubs, or deliveries, excepting newspapers, and no football or cricket team. However, it has become a pleasant retirement area for those who wish to live out their years in the peace and quiet of the south Shropshire countryside.

It wasn't always so! There were once thriving hamlets and townships; communities touched by the upheaval of the Norman Conquest, the lusts of a Plantagenet king, and the greedy grasping hands of the mediaeval Church. Lords and ladies, farmers and peasants, wealthy landowners and wartime evacuees, all have played their part in the history of Stanton Lacy.

During these writings I have had difficulty in obtaining information concerning some areas of the parish. Some records are not that reliable and in others contradict each other. However, I have written this book with the conviction that it is correct as far as can be proven. My intentions have not been to offend anyone, but if there are those that are offended, please accept my apologies: the offence was not intentional.

Clifford Smout
September 1998

CHAPTER I

Staunton: 'Stone Town'

At the time of the Norman Conquest in 1066, Staunton was held by the Saxon Earl Siward, who at that time was one of the chief landowners in what was to become the County of Shropshire.

After the Conquest, Roger de Lacy, first son of Walter de Lacy, was said to be holding the Manors of Staunton (subsequently Staunton Lacy), Aldon, Stokesay, Cleobury North and Hopton under the Earl of Shrewsbury, Roger de Montgomery. Roger de Lacy's name has also been linked with the building of the castle and the laying out of the town at Ludlow, then in a corner of the Manor of Staunton, though I have my own doubts as to this.

The Domesday Survey in 1086 was a correct taxation record of these counties that had been conquered by the Normans. But one translator of the Domesday Survey and another may arrive at different interpretations, and affairs are complicated on the Welsh border where not all landholdings are included, only those which were taxable—marcher lordships were able to create their own governments and laws, and only great matters of state were enforced by the monarch in their territory.

To try and arrive at an accurate account of the de Lacy family one must go back some 15 years before the Conquest to the reign of Edward the Confessor. Edward was born and brought up in Normandy, and was said to be more Norman than English in his thinking and deeds. In around 1050 he allowed Norman noblemen to live in parts of England, granting them lands and power, notably along the Welsh Marches in the counties of Herefordshire, Cheshire and Shropshire, where they were expected to, and did, help in the never-ending struggle against the Welsh. However, they did also excite the hostility of the Saxons. In 1051 the Anglo-Saxon Chronicles recorded:

> The Foreigners have built castles in Herefordshire in Earl Sweyne's territory and have inflicted all injury and insults they could on the King's men in that region.

These 'Norman' pre-Conquest castles were Richard's Castle, Ewyas Harold and probably that at Hereford. Ewyas Harold may have been the castle of Owen Pentecost, mentioned in the Anglo Saxon Chronicle (D version). The 'Harold' could have been the son of Earl; Ralph who was the nephew of Edward the Confessor and the first Earl of Hereford.

After the Conquest but before Domesday, William I created three Earldoms along the Welsh March. The Earldom of Chester he gave to his trusted friend, Hugh de Avranches. His cousin, William Fitzosbern, was created Earl of Hereford, while another trusted friend, Roger de Montgomery was made Earl of Shrewsbury. These three Earldoms acted as separate little Kingdoms from that of the crown—like all marcher lordships they had their own laws, and were only responsible to the king in great matters of state. Their freedom of action was often the cause of tension with the crown in subsequent generations, the chance for the final removal of their independent powers coming when Edward Mortimer became king as Edward IV in 1461, during the Wars of the Roses, so amalgamating many marcher lordships with the crown. The Act of Union with Wales which followed soon after the Tudors came to power a couple of decades later completed the process.

Roger de Montgomery, Earl of Shrewsbury, built Corfham Castle (OS 525849), now in the Parish of Diddlebury, around which Roger created a great manor. In 1087 Roger was granted Ludlow and the Vale of Corf by William II, and the tithes of Corfham were passed to Shrewsbury Abbey. At this time, the Vale of Corf which included Staunton, which only became Stanton Lacy some 170 years after Domesday. Hence the possible confusion as to the role that Roger de Lacy played.

The House of Lacy

Walter de Lacy was created Lord of Ewias or Ewyas after the Conquest, holding many manors under the Earl of Hereford, including the Golden Valley. This name, I fear, is a mistake on the part of the Normans. The Welsh named the valley 'dwr' pronounced 'dore' which is Welsh for water. The Normans called it 'd'or', pronounced 'dore' the French for golden. The River Dore runs through the entire length of the valley, which is still known as the Golden Valley.

Though Walter de Lacy was settled by the Conqueror at Ewyas Lacy, he later had his caput, the centre of his lordship, at Weobley, both of which are in Herefordshire. Weobley was subsequently created a borough (it had a market by 1272), and the de Lacy family built priories at Wormsley and Aconbury. The Priory of Llanthony was started by Hugh de Lacy, second son of Walter. The de Lacy Manors of Holm Lacy, Stoke Lacy, Mansell Lacy and Ewias Lacy still survive in name to this present day. From their arrival in this country until their demise around 1384, the de Lacys looked upon Herefordshire as their adopted home, their interests in Shropshire being very small in comparison.

Walter de Lacy played a key role in the defence of the Marches against the Welsh, especially after William Fitzosbern, Earl of Hereford, was slain in Flanders on February 20th, 1071. He subsequently also helped to crush the revolt of Earl William's son, Roger. As a result, Walter was given custody of some of Earl William's son's forfeited estates. In addition, Walter was responsible for building St Peter's Church in Hereford, and died on March 27th, 1085, when he fell from its walls. His lands then passed to his eldest son Roger. He in turn was banished in 1095 by William II, who had taken the Crown after his father's death from wounds received at the siege of Mantes on 9th September, 1087. The manors that Roger had succeeded to on the death of Walter then passed to his younger brother Hugh, and included land in Berkshire, Herefordshire, Worcestershire, Gloucestershire and a few small manors in Shropshire. It seems that Earl Fitzosbern's second son, another Hugh, never regained his father's lands, indeed it is unclear what happened to him. The profusion of Rogers, Hughs, Williams, Gilberts, Henrys and Walters in the eleventh and twelfth centuries has certainly added confusion to the history of this period.

Though the de Lacys also held lands at Clifford, they didn't hold the castle. At the time of Domesday Clifford Castle, which stands above the River Wye to the east of Hay-on-Wye in Herefordshire, was held by Ralph de Tosny. The survey records that the castle was built by Earl William Fitzosbern on waste land that belonged to Browning before 1066. Roger de Lacy held some lands in the castelry, but these were also waste at the time of Domesday. A daughter of Ralph de Tosny married Richard fitz Ponce, and their second son, Walter took the surname of Clifford. Why they chose the name Clifford instead of Ponce is unclear, perhaps Ponce was not to their liking, though then it could not have had the connotations that the name would have today. The Cliffords subsequently brought their name to Shropshire when the Castle of

A few mounds and part of the dry moat is all that remains of Roger de Montgomery's Corfham Castle in the parish of Diddlebury which was gifted to the de Cliffords in 1178

Corfham was granted to Walter de Clifford, son of the De Ponces, by Henry II in 1178. This gift was in exchange for the favours of fair Rosamund, daughter of Walter de Clifford.

As for records concerning Ludlow and Staunton, they are contradictory. Roger de Lacy is generally believed to be responsible for the building of Ludlow Castle—this is the general opinion within the history of Ludlow. Roger de Lacy may have started to build the castle around 1085 a year before Domesday, and the year in which his father Walter died. But in 1087, one year after Domesday, we learn that William II, William Rufus, second son of William the Conqueror, has given Lude 'and all of the Vale of Corf' including Staunton, to Roger de Montgomery, with an understanding that the said Roger, Earl of Shrewsbury will build a strong fortress and town around the castle of Ludlow. This came about two years after Roger de Lacy was said to have been building the castle of Ludlow and eight years before his banishment by William II. In my reckoning the entry in the Domesday book refers to Roger de Montgomery not Roger de Lacy, when Staunton is mentioned. Nevertheless, the guide to *Historic Ludlow* says 'Between 1086 and 1094 ... Roger [de Lacy] began to build a castle on a well protected site in the south western corner of the manor [that of Staunton].' David Lloyd's *Ludlow Castle, A History and A Guide*, says 'The de Lacys and their heirs retained the lordship [that of Staunton] until the late 13th century', though recognizing that at times it was in royal hands, and in the wars in Stephen's reign (1135-1154) was held by Joyce de Dinam, an enemy of the de Lacys.

The de Lacys did hold a Manor of Staunton under the earls of Hereford at Domesday, but this Staunton lay near Llanvihangel Crucorney (OS 314216) now in Wales, but then on the English side of the ever shifting border.

The house of Lacy seems to have had its ups and downs through history, and there are periods when the name is difficult to even find, this may be due to there being a period in their history when there were few sons born to the family. However, in 1233 we find that Gilbert de Lacy had become Earl of Lincoln on his marriage to a niece of the late Earl Ranulf de Blunderville who had died childless. The de Lacys held this Earldom from 1233 until 1348 when it is written that the de Lacy family died out. The reason for their demise is said to have been due to intermarriage, which brought infertility and insanity. It is possible that the female line may have lived on, but it would take many years of research to prove or disprove this. For example, take the old village of Whychecott or Witchcot. in Staunton Parish. In 1532 Witchcot was handed, not sold, to Hamond Whychecott of Dunstan, Lincolnshire. Could he be a descendant of the de Lacys of Lincoln?

'Staunton Lacy' is first mentioned as such in 1255, 14 years after the death of Walter de Lacy, last of the line, or so we are told. The de Lacy or Lacy family had several branches in the 13th and 14th centuries. I have mentioned Gilbert, Earl of Lincoln, and Walter holding Ludlow, another brother William became Earl of Denbigh. Around 1230 Llewelyn the Great, Prince of Gwynedd, tired of fighting against the English, and trying to bring peace and stability to Wales married his son and four daughters to marcher families in the hope that this would be achieved. His son, also Llewelyn, married an heiress of the De Breose family, Helen married John, Earl of Chester, Margaret married John de Breose (after his death marrying Walter Clifford), Gwladus married first Reginald de Breose, secondly Ralph de Mortimer. The third daughter, Gwenllian, married William de Lacy who was granted the Earldom of Denbigh by Llewelyn the Great.

Llewelyn died in 1240, and his plans had been in vain, for many more battles were fought along the border before peace finally came. The Welsh rebellion of 1280 destroyed that part of the de Lacy family which held the Earldom of Denbigh, and in 1282 the land was granted to Henry de Lacy, Earl of Lincoln.

Walter de Lacy, the last of the branch of the family who held Staunton, died in 1241. The manor of Stanton Lacy then passed to his granddaughter

Maud who had married Geoffrey de Geneville, a member of a powerful north Herefordshire family. Geoffrey and Maud had one son Peter who had, for some unrecorded reason, replaced Geoffrey in holding Stanton Lacy in Geoffrey's own lifetime.

On Peter's death he left three daughters, Johanna born February 2nd 1286, Beatrix born 1287 and Matilda born 1291. Beatrix and Matilda became nuns at the convent of Aconbury, their aunt being prioress at that time, having replaced Kathleen de Lacy. Johanna inherited the Manor of Stanton Lacy and carried it with her into the hands of the de Mortimers on her marriage to Roger de Mortimer, first Earl of March. The de Mortimer family were subsequently responsible for the enlargement and rebuilding of the Church of St. Peter, Stanton Lacy. Roger de Mortimer was executed for high treason in 1330 by the young Edward III, having essentially been ruling the kingdom for a number of years with Edward's mother, Queen Isabella.

Before Domesday two thirds of the tithes of Stanton Lacy had gone to St. Peters in Hereford, after Domesday to Gloucester Abbey, and from 1290 after the crushing of Llewelyn, to Llanthony Priory, church records referring to Stanton Lacy as Stanton Llanthony as late as 1733.

The Manor

We must not confuse a manor with a parish. A manor could be a small or large part of a parish, but usually referred to the part that had been cultivated for many years and consisted of the most fertile lands and managed forests or woods. Much of the parish of Stanton Lacy belonged to different owners under different overlords throughout its history.

The last record of the Manor when it was held by the family of Geneville on the death of Peter de Geneville on June 8th 1292, records that the Manor of Stanton Lacy consisted of:

> A Capital Messuage and Garden = 20s. 4 carucates of land value £16, 30 acres of meadow = £3 6s 8d. A watermill = £1 10s 0d, a vivary 2s 0d, 10 acres of pasture land 10s 0d and 80 acres of woodland 5s 0d. Rents £10. Pleas and Perquisites of the manor Court = £2. Total £34 13 8d.

From this one may gather what was termed as a 'Manor'! These could, of course, grow or diminish at any time. The Manor, however large or small, always included the advowson of the parish church.

CHAPTER II

Stanton Lacy in Decline?

From the time of the execution of Roger de Mortimer in 1330, Stanton Lacy must have declined very quickly. The Assessments of the Ninth in 1341—a taxation record which adjusted parish tax assessments—taxed Stanton Lacy at £7 8s. 8d. Most parishes were assessed at £10. The register declares that:

> much of the Parish of Stanton Lacy is waste and untilled, the corn has suffered from tempest and there has been a general murrain among the sheep.

Yet we also gather that 'Shropshire wool' was fetching the highest prices ever on the Flemish wool market.

Stanton Lacy remained on a downward path. In 1349 the Bubonic Plague arrived, the 'Black Death' introduced and spread by rats from southern India. The plague quickly spread throughout the country, and whilst on average half the villages' population died, the death tolls were far higher in the urban areas. From the records we gather that what passed for a village was an agglomeration of filthy hovels infested with rats, mice, lice and fleas, whose inhabitants wore the same threadbare collection of rags for months on end, had bodies that crawled with vermin and drank from the streams that served their cattle, pigs and other animals. It is written that the worshippers at the church of St. Peter, Stanton Lacy, had the floor strawed for the purpose of kneeling.

Further outbreaks of the plague in 1361—1369, 1371 and 1375 cut the national population from 4.5 million to around 2 million. It was during these terrible times that several villages in the parish became lost or abandoned. Ye

Ye, Lower Hayton, Witchcot, Postern and the Cuphelmston, now called Camp Ring. Coupled with lack of manpower due to the plague, the heavy taxation needed for King Edward III to continue the French wars made it impossible for a living to be made in community farming. As Statutes were passed to also try and hold down wages, people fled the land, leaving it to return to waste.

By the year 1540, the national population had climbed back to 5.5 million, by 1801 to 8.8 million, and to a staggering 32 million by 1901. The high rise in the population in the century up until 1901 was not due to the better health of the people, but is recorded as being accredited to the fall in the marriage age, and larger families due to improvements in wages and conditions.

The Manor of Stanton Lacy should not have been affected by these hard times being a tenure under the Crown until 1561 when the Queen granted it to Robert Thorpe and Francis Baldrowe and the heirs of Frances. But in the following year, 1562, licence was given to Edward Russell to sell the Manor to Simon Clare and Agnes, his wife, and their heirs. Simon died in 1580, his son Francis held the Manor in 1583, his son, also Francis was baptised in Stanton Lacy church in 1606. In this same year, Francis sold it to one Bonham Norton who was the Royal Printer and who had bought much property in the county. In 1609 the Crown had repossessed part of the manorial rights of Stanton Lacy. Bonham Norton sold his part of the Manor to Elizabeth, widow of Sir William Craven in 1624, and this remained in the Craven family for over two centuries.

The Cravens were to become the Earls of Craven, owning much of south Shropshire. When they sold their interests in this area in 1862, the village of Stanton Lacy was purchased by the Herberts of Oakley Park, whilst the Powells of Sutton Court in the parish of Diddlebury bought part of the Manor. Other areas of the parish that did not belong to the Cravens, but were in the hands of the Cornwalls or Herbert families were sold off around the turn of this century. The Heynes family, then the Pearces, followed by the Pearce Halls and later the Rouse Boughton family held Downton for many years. The Herbert family, the earls of Powys, still own the mineral rights over much of the parish.

CHAPTER III

The Earls of Craven

The purchase of the Manor of Stanton Lacy by the Craven family brought about a dramatic change. The Cravens appeared to be a forward looking family. Many farms and cottages were built creating work for masons and carpenters who moved in from other parts of the county or country. Quarrymen, woodmen and carters were needed to supply stone and timber to the large building programme. Limeburners, trenchers and charcoal burners, all found work within the parish and their descendants still live there.

At the time of The Great Enclosure Acts of 1750-1850 some 200,000 miles of new hedges were planted throughout the county. This was equal in distance to all the hedges planted in the previous 500 years in the County of Shropshire.

During the Enclosure Act years turkeys were farmed in large numbers. Women and children were employed in the gathering of seeds and berries—crabapples, haws, hips, sloes, dogwood, acorns, beech nuts, maple seeds, elderberries—to feed along with other ingredients to the turkeys. Meanwhile the men were employed to dig ditches, throwing up the resulting soil into parallel ridges. These ridges were made firm, the tops flattened, and when settled, the top two inches were forked over until a fine tilth was achieved. The women and children spread the turkey muck along these ridges, covering it with fine soil topped with branches of gorse. The seeds within the turkey muck germinated, resulting in infant hedges. (It must be stressed that rabbits then were not the problem that they are today. Many were farmed in warrens within an area of the estates. Those that did escape were kept in check by a hungry population.)

'Hoopers Rule' would instruct one to measure out a 30 yard strip of hedge, counting the different species contained within it. Each species would then represent one hundred years in the age of the hedge. I have carried out these instructions on many occasions, finding as many as 10 different species in a 30 yard strip, making the age of the hedge over 1,000 years—but I have known before the experiment was carried out, that the hedge had been planted between 1750 and 1850.

Despite all the hard work that went into enclosing the land, we find that about the same time as the first newly planted hedges and hedgerow timber were growing away, many were already being grubbed out. The House of Commons Journal of 1792 states:

> The grubbing up of hedges is become general and the growth of timber in them is thereby totally destroyed, owing to the great price given for corn since the bounty took place for exporting corn and beer, which gives every farmer encouragement to grub up hedge-rows and convert them into corn land.

Much the same practice has taken place recently, with the taxpayer paying towards the cost. Here I must stress that one cannot blame the farmer for accepting these handouts; many of them would welcome a free market. Now hedgerows receive some protection from the planning system, whilst land under the Countryside Stewardship scheme or in Environmentally Sensitive Areas (E.S.A.s) benefits from grants to ensure the land is managed less intensively.

Under the Earls of Craven and the Earls of Powys, Stanton Lacy once again became a very successful parish. At the first full census of 1841 we find that it consisted of 7,765 acres of land plus 30 acres of water, with 1,540 inhabitants. Sadly, it is noted that 146 of these were in the Union Workhouse at Gravelhill, Ludlow, then part of the parish.

The Townships in the Parish of Stanton Lacy 1841

	Land in Acres	No. of Houses	Inhabitants
Downton	765	17	90
Hayton Upper with Hayton Bent	935	53	256
Hayton Lower	535	24	104
Rock Green	735	32	134
Wootton	544	9	65
East hamlet	734	4	24
West hamlet	650	9	65

From the above one may notice that the census makes no mention of Stanton Lacy Village, proving as I have written on several occasions, that the records were not very accurate at that time.

Totalling up the acreage and number of inhabitants we arrive at the following: 4,898 acres with 738 inhabitants plus 146 in the Union Workhouse = 884 inhabitants. These figures would leave Stanton Lacy village and its surrounding area as being 2,867 acres with a population of 656, roughly 4.5 persons per acre and crammed into approximately 20 houses. This figure is of course incorrect, but I have entered it to prove my previous statement that parish records were not very accurate at that time in our history.

During these times, agriculture was the main industry as indeed it is currently—but it was not the settled, nursed, industry of today. Hard times, diseases among livestock, bad harvests, severe winters, and drought, were then born by the farmer, not shared with the hard pressed taxpayer. Because of this the owners and tenants were regularly changing. To get a truer picture we can look at the 'Directories' of the parish.

1841

Stanton Lacy	Herbert Blakeway (F)	Stanton Cottage Farm		*
	John and Richard Evans (F)	Manor Farm		*
	John Davies, Blacksmith	Smithy		
	Henry Edwards, Victualler	Craven Arms Inn		
	Richard Evans, Butcher	Shop (?)		
	Edward Farmer, (F) & Shopkeeper	(?)		
	John Hotchkiss (F)	Woodlands	*	#
Downton	Sir W.E.Rouse-Boughton	Landowner		#
	Thomas Hotchkiss (F)	Home Farm	*	#
Wootton	William Blakeway (F)	Whitehouse	*	
	Josiah Meredith, Miller	Mill		
East Hamlet	William Patrick (F)	?	*	
West Hamlet	Thomas Lloyd (F)	Langley	*	
	John Mellings (F)	The Pools	*	#
	Deborah Sanders (F)	Ruckley		
	John Sanders (F)	The Holt		
	William Small (F)	Aintree	*	

Lower Hayton	Richard Coston (F)	Whitehouse	*	
	Sarah Coston (F)	?		
	Samuel Weaver (F)	The Hopes		
	Samuel Weaver, Beerhouse Keeper	The Hopes		
Upper Hayton & Bent	Edward Burgess (F)		*	
	Thomas Smout (F)		*	#
	William Price (F)			
	Rev. Lancelot Dixon (F)	Dixon Place		
Rock Green	William Gardener (F)	Bache	*	
	James Harding, Victualler	Raven Inn		
	James Hince, Timber Merchant			
	James Price, Gas Works Manager			
	Ellias Rollings, Coach & Jobbing Smith			
	William Russell, Governor, Union Workhouse			
	William Thompson, Victualler	Greyhound Inn		
	James Watkins, Stone & Marble Mason			

(F) Farmer
* Over 150 acres
\# Direct descendants still living or owning land within the Parish.

By the year 1881 things had changed dramatically. In 1879 a Local Government Board Order transferred all the detached areas of Stanton Lacy parish to neighbouring parishes, *i.e.* Bromfield, Onibury, Bitterley, and also into the confines of Ludlow when the East Hamlet became a parish, thus shrinking the parish by some 40%.

Census 1881

Stanton Lacy	Rev. L.R.C. Bagot	Vicar	
	Sir C.H. Rouse-Boughton		Downton
	B. Beddoes	(F)	Woodlands
	H. Beddoes	(F)	Stocking
	J. Bengry	Shoemaker	Hayton Bent
	Mrs. M. Bengry	School	Hayton Bent 'Chapel'
	T. Bengry	Butcher	Lower Hayton
	H. Bishop	Blacksmith	Hayton Bent
	J. Brookes	(F)	Lower Hayton
	T. Brown	(F)	New House
	W. Daneford	(F)	Langley

J. Davis	Blacksmith	Stanton Lacy
J. Dixon	(F)	Hayton Bent
C. Downs	Victualler	New Inn, Lower Hayton
A. Edwards	Overseer	Hayton Bent
F. Edwards	(F)	?
R. Edwards	(F)	?
Job Evans	Cowkeeper	Downton
R. Evans	(F)	Hopton Hall
J. Evison	Wheelwright & Carpenter	Stanton Lacy
Mrs. M. Farmer	(F)	
R. Fletcher	(F) & Shop Keeper	Hayton Bent
T. Hall	(F)	Lower Hayton
W. Hall	(F)	Hayton Bent
G. Hayhurst	(F)	Witchcot
G. Howells	(F)	Upper Hayton
W. Jones	Shoe Maker	Stanton Lacy
T. Marston	(F)	Upper Hayton
J. Matthews	(F) & Shop Keeper	Lower Hayton
T. Mellings	(F) & Waywarden	Pools
W. Meredith	(F)	The Holt
W. Millichamp	(F)	Downton
T. Norgrove	(F)	Hopton
E. Palmer	(F)	Downton
Mrs. E. Potter	(F)	Upper Hayton
J. Powell	Cowkeeper	?
R. Reece	(F)	Hopton Gate
J. Rowe	Wheelwright, Shoeing & General Smith, Agricultural Implement Repairer	California
H. Sambrook	(F) and relieving officer for No.2 district Ludlow Union	Hayton Bent
S. Sankey	Shoemaker	Hope
G. Slater	(F)	Upper Hayton
R. & H. Whiteman	(F)	Lower Hayton
G. Williams	(F)	Hope
A.C. Bowskill	Postmaster &Schoolmaster	Stanton Lacy
John Evison	Carrier	Stanton Lacy
Mrs. Eliza Brookes	Carrier	Lower Hayton

From this census we gather that very few families mentioned in the survey of 1841 were still farming or trading within the parish.

The 1914-18 war also brought about a further upheaval within our parish, much as it must have done in parishes throughout the land.

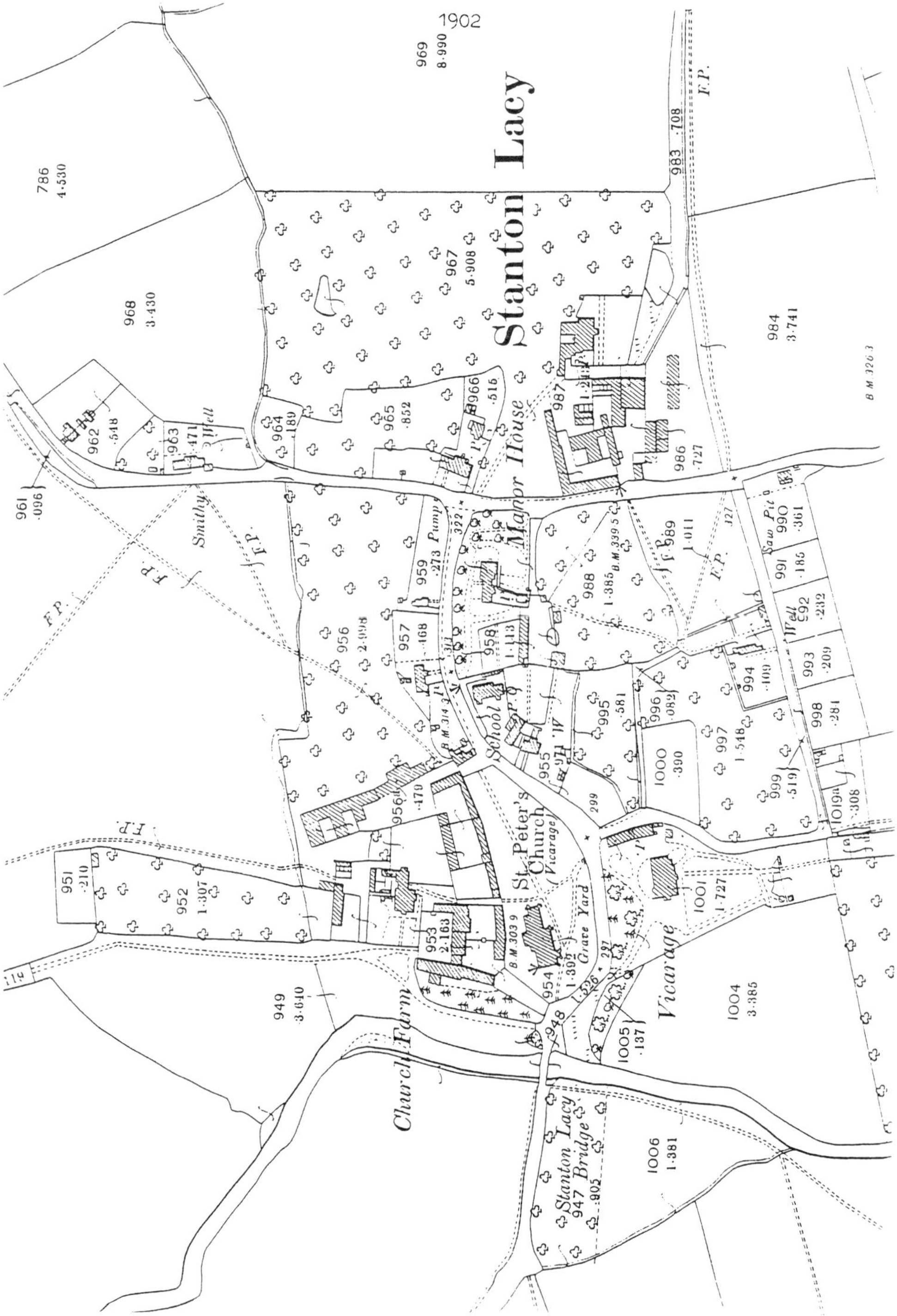
1902
Stanton Lacy
Manor House
St. Peter's Church (Vicarage)
Grave Yard
School
Church Farm
Vicarage
Stanton Lacy Bridge
Smithy
Pump
Saw Pit
Well
F.P.

Please bear with me in listing the survey carried out in 1923.

Stanton Lacy Parish - 1923

Rev. R.R. Armitage M.A., D.S.O.	Vicar	
P. Harris	Gentleman	Manor House
Sir W. Rouse-Boughton		Downton
R. Bailey	Smallholder	Potters Farm
W. Bailey	Gamekeeper	Downton
Mrs. C. Brereton	(F)	Langley
J. Brown	(F)	New House
T. Brown	(F)	Witchcott
C. Bryan	(F)	Mansion House
Mrs. H. Cox	(F)	Hayton Bent
T. Downs	(F)	Manor Farm
R. Downs	(F)	Woodlands
G. Edwards	Smallholder	Hayton Bent
R. Evison	Carpenter	Stanton Lacy
A. Fletcher	(F)	Hayton Bent
Miss C. Fletcher	Shopkeeper	Hayton Bent
J. Furber	Smallholder	Hayton Bent
E. Green	(F)	Hopes Farm
R. Green	(F)	Hopton Hall
W. Harris	Smallholder	The Hope
W. Henner	Dairyman	North Cottage, Lower Hayton
Mrs. C. Holland	Smallholder	The Hope
D. James	(F)	Coppice Farm
D. John	(F)	Church Farm *
G. Jones	Blacksmith	Stanton Lacy
W. Jones	Shoemaker & Parish Clerk	Stanton Lacy
E. Key	(F)	Hayton Bent
W. Keysell	(F)	Hayton Bent
J. Mellings	(F)	The Pools
J. Morgan	Cowkeeper	Hayton Bent
A. Norgrove	(F)	Lodge Farm (Hope)
E. Norgrove	(F)	Hayton Bent
J. Norgrove	(F)	Hopton
J. Nott	Landlord	New Inn
T. Price	Cowkeeper	Upper Hayton
H. Reece	(F)	Hopton Gate
C. Richards	(F)	Hope

H. Rowe	Wheelwright	California
E. Teague	(F)	Upper Hayton
J. Wadeley	Postman & Cowkeeper	Hayton Bent
Mrs. C. Wadeley	Postmistress	Hayton Bent
C. Wait	(F)	Rose Farm
E. Went	Blacksmith	Hayton Bent
E. Wilde	Smallholder	Hopton Gate
F. Williams	Smallholder	Hope
Miss M. Williams	School Mistress	School, Hayton Bent

To eliminate the risk of offending certain families, I would point out that the census only listed those families who were carrying out a business, or farming within the parish; cottagers and working families were not mentioned.

The Sherry family have lived in or around the parish since the 1460s, the Pickens from 1600, the Easthopes from around the 1520s and the Smout family since at least 1365.

As mentioned earlier, in 1862, the Earls of Craven sold their interests. Much of Lower and Upper Hayton land was bought by the Powell family of Sutton Court. Other areas were sold to the Clive family of Oakly Park, Bromfield. The Earls of Powys disposed of their holdings; often selling to tenant farmers who could afford to buy. It must be mentioned that the Earls of Powys sold the land but reserved the mineral rights which they still own.

The P.G. Holder Estates bought a great deal of property around the turn of the century. By the year 1911 much of this land had been offered for sale to the sitting tenants in the parishes of Stanton Lacy, Diddlebury, Clee St. Margaret, Tugford and Stoke St. Milborough. Those lands within Stanton Lacy and surrounding parishes, not sold to tenants, were purchased by the Church Commissioners in 1940. They in turn sold out to sitting tenants in the 1960s: their lands not disposed of in this way, were sold to Viscount Boyne Estates, creating the present Viscount Boyne Peaton Estate.

From a survey carried out around 1925, farming and the associated country industries were once again in decline throughout the land, partly due to poor prices and many families moving to the towns to gain a better standard of living and the changing attitudes between farmer and workman. (This was brought about by the men returning from the 1914-18 war, having gained an insight into a better world than that they had left in 1914—that is to say that they had been in the company of others from all walks of life, who had told them stories of their own working conditions in the towns and cities). Many of the men returned bitter and resentful of those that had not answered the call, or had escaped conscription in some way. These non-serving men were termed 'Mixen Snipers'. 'The Royal Standbacks', 'The Fireside Lancers' and other such names. Bitterness was felt by families who had lost husbands, fathers or sons. Many life-long feuds started in this way.

A reduction in the agricultural wage in the 1920s, due it is said to poor returns, accelerated the decline in the farming industry. By the 1930s some areas of farmland had returned to scrub and woodland. Things went from bad to worse. A general strike was to hit the British Isles in the 1930s, bringing with it times of great hardship for everyone.

Europe was in the same state as Britain. If we look back in history we will find that when the coffers are empty 'War!' has often been the answer. The 1939-45 war brought about conditions completely opposite to those that had existed during World War I. Conditions in fact improved for those people living in the Shires; everyone was employed and so received a wage. It was against the law to refuse to work, even those people farming—smallholders were forced to work so many days each week on the larger farms. Agriculture received a huge boost, as everyone pulled together in their efforts to make the country self-sufficient.

The War-Ag was founded. This movement brought in heavy machinery and cleared huge areas of neglected land that had grown nothing but brambles, gorse and bracken for the past 25 years. One of the worst examples of neglect in Stanton Lacy could be seen at The Woodlands Farm, where 50% of this 365 acre holding had been taken over by scrub. With much hard work and forward thinking by Mr. John Pugh, the new tenant, and his sons, Francis and John, and great help from his workmen and the War-Ag, this neglected area was once again turned into good fertile farmland, growing wheat, barley, oats and much needed potato crops. John Pugh's grandson Graham, with his wife and young family now farm Woodlands Farm, a tidy well managed unit, a far cry from the overgrown mess the family found when they took over the property in the spring of 1942.

Many of the dwellings on the large farms and estates had not improved at anytime in their history. Nothing besides a new thatch had been added since the Earls of Craven and Powys had had them built 200 years before. With the improvements in conditions the owners were given an ultimatum: repair—or we condemn them. With the money not forthcoming for much needed repairs, many houses were demolished. This trend continued up until the 1980s when a boom in the buying of derelict country cottages and turning them into larger homes became fashionable. This new trend helped to tidy up those derelict properties that had been an eyesore within the parish.

I can remember 37 parish dwellings which were standing in my childhood and were demolished before anyone had a chance to purchase them. By jumping the gun the owners lost thousands of pounds which could have been made from selling the derelict properties, had they been left standing until the 1980s.

Stanton Lacy is now home to many retired people. Many of the old family names have died out, or moved away, as is true of parishes throughout the Shires. There are just eleven family names left who were here at the time of my birth. Two of these families are childless, a further three have only produced daughters, so their names will also die out. This will soon leave just six families keeping their old family name within Stanton Lacy parish.

CHAPTER IV

Stanton Lacy Village

The village of Stanton Lacy was once high on the list of the prettiest villages in the county. Today, one would be hardpressed to find a more rundown neglected village in the West Midlands. Farming, together with poor drainage has taken its toll, turning the once pretty lanes into a sea of mud in winter and a dustbath in high summer. Sadly, for many of the residents, it is to all intents and purposes a village still run under the old feudal system. No one is forcing this rule upon the village, but many have lived for so long paying homage, and bootlicking, that they can now do nothing about their plight, though self-administered it may be.

Everywhere there is the stench of silage. This stench gets into every house and building. Those of us who have had the misfortune to enter a 'Cholera Village' will know what I mean.

If no one complains about the destruction of their once lovely village, then nothing will ever be done to halt its decline!

The time when the so-called 'Lord of the Manor' endeavoured to bluff his poorer neighbours into a belief that his privilege was beyond question or dispute, is long past. Their antisocial attitudes were mostly founded on a superiority complex which has no foundations and are unacceptable as we approach the 21st century.

The Church of St. Peter

Much has been written about this lovely old church. My scant knowledge of religicn could add nothing to it. But one does wonder why, when reading through these writings, so much has been written about certain members of the church and parish, including drunken and murdering parsons! Here are monuments that proclaim what fine upstanding people lie buried here, but the epitaphs have been composed by close family members, so are not too accurate in some cases.

With all these epitaphs both inside and outside the church it is sad to note that there is seldom a mention of the saddest monument of all. The War Memorial which records the names of 22 men of the parish who answered the call, paying the ultimate price during the 1914-18 war.

Farewell to barn and stack and tree
Farewell to Severn shore.
My friends, look you last on me,
For I come home no more.

The smoke blows o'er the trenches still
By now the blood is dried
And I among the dead lie still
With a bullet in my side.

Oh here's a bloody hand to shake,
And oh, man here's good-bye,
We'll sweat no more, on scythe and rake,
My bloody hands and I.

Long for me the rick will wait,
And long will wait the fold,
For I stand at oblivion's gate,
And never shall grow old. (*Anon.*)

The War Memorial

Inside the church there are to be found the names of a further 101 men who served in World War I and returned more or less intact. The Roll of Honour includes my own father, Andrew Smout, who served with the Royal Horse Artillery, but sadly there is no mention of his mother, who saw active service in Flanders, and was among the few women decorated for bravery while serving with the Queen Mary's Army Auxiliary Corps which had been founded to bring the British Army up to strength, their losses being so great.

These women were said to have been a frightening sight as they cursed, coaxed and thrashed their teams of terrified horses and mules drawing the ammunition wagons and ambulances up to the front line. Many teams and drivers were lost. Once a team went down very little could be done. They sank

Top Left: My great uncles, brothers Tom and Dick., who served with the K.S.L.I. Thomas Lewis (left) was killed at Arras, 28 March 1918. Richard Lewis (right) was lost without trace, presumed killed, 9 August 1915, during the defence of the Ypres Salient

Top Right: Pte. James Gwilt, 'Uncle Jim', of the Worcestershire Regiment with wife Fanny (née Smout) and son Walter. Jim survived the war, but died two days after the armistice was signed, in the Dourcourt military hospital. He is buried in St Margarets churchyard, Abdon

Left: W.W. Brown, my mother's half-brother, my 'Uncle Walter', who served with the Royal Horse Artillery. He died aged 19 at Ypres in 1917

into the shell holes, helped on by the shelling and the ever moving suffocating mud. Grandmother's citation hangs on the wall of Rock Cottage, The Bullring, where she was born in 1874. It is signed by Winston Churchill, Secretary of State for War, on behalf of King George V.

Father and Grandmother served in the same field of battle. There can be very few cases where this has happened before or since. It is a great pity that the Rev. Lewis Bagot did not see fit to include a woman's name in the Roll of Honour. Perhaps he considered that women were not worth mentioning way back in 1919; but then 45,000 British women who saw active service would no doubt have disagreed with him!

A sad reminder of unhappy days. Richard Green's gravestone in a British military cemetery near Munster. Richard was taken prisoner on the Somme and died in a prisoner of war camp in 1918

Two names of men were added to the War Memorial after World War II:

Thomas E. Bailey
of the Potters Farm,
killed in 1944, serving with the Warwickshire Yeomanry
aged 27 years
Eric Christopher Cornes
of No.1 Hayton Bent,
also killed in 1944, serving with the Gloucestershire Regiment,
aged 18 years.

Here dead we lie because we did not choose,
To live and shame the land from which we sprung,
Life, to be sure, is nothing much to lose,
But young men think it is, and we were young. (*Anon.*)

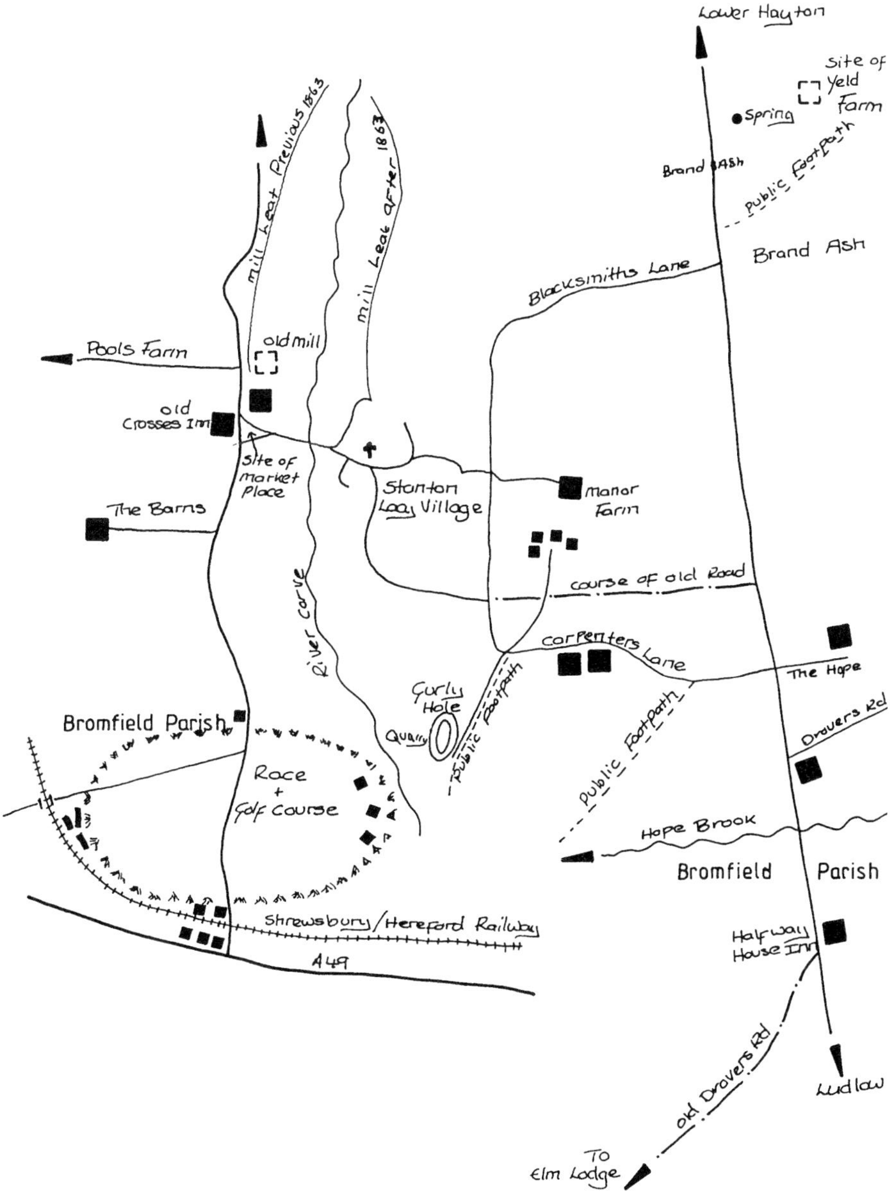

Map showing the area around Stanton Lacy village

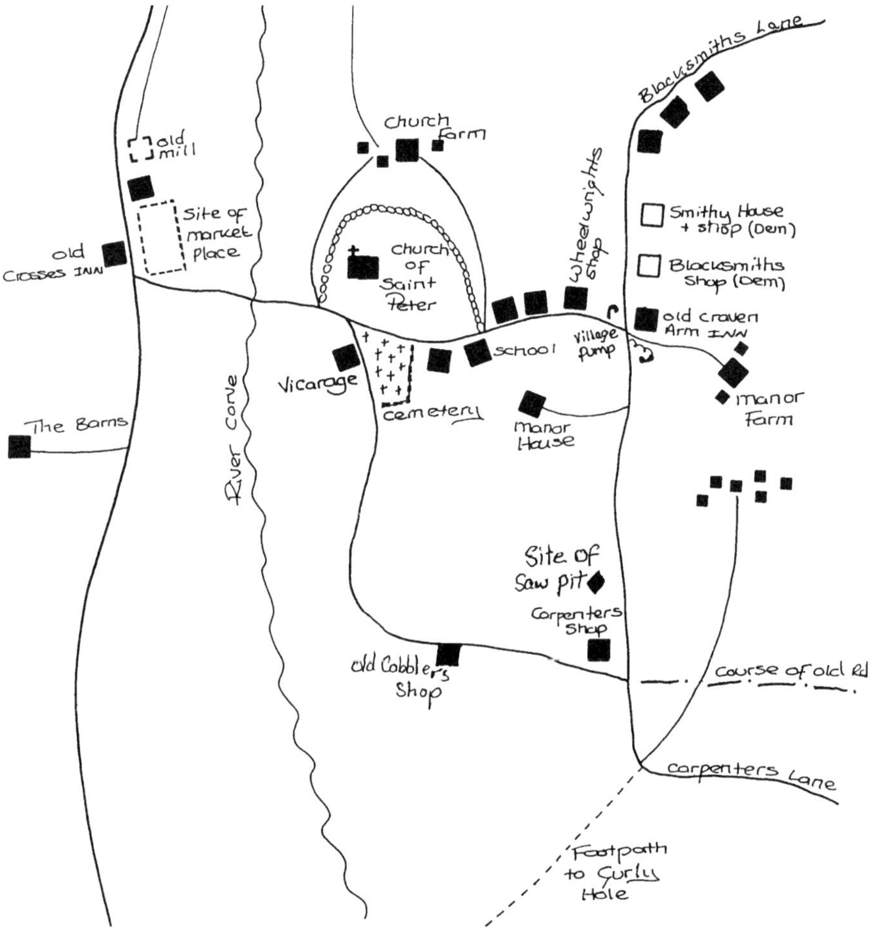

Map showing Stanton Lacy village itself

Church Farm

Church Farm is first mentioned in the census of 1901. Whilst the farm buildings are of some considerable age, the house, however, dates from around 1820, though there is no mention of this building in any of the ten year censuses from 1841 until 1901. However, there is Stanton Cottage Farm mentioned in the census from 1841 onwards, and here we must tread most carefully. There are some records that suggest that the black and white cottage opposite the entrance to the Manor House was in fact Stanton Cottage, the farmer farming Church Farm from here. I do not think that this building was large enough to have been a farmhouse from which such a large farm could have been run. All things like buttermaking, brewing, bacon and ham curing were then run from the farmhouse, and these chores needed a large area in which the small army of servants could work and live. Without doubt, this fine house must have been the Stanton Cottage Farm which is mentioned, changing its name to Church Farm House between the 1891 and 1901 census.

The Blakeway family farmed Stanton Cottage Farm for many years under the Earl of Craven; this same Blakeway family also ran Stanton Lacy Mill.

☆ ☆ ☆ ☆

Moving westwards we pass over the River Corve by way of an ugly narrow roadbridge built in 1878 to replace the old bridge built in 1760. Before this, one crossed by fording the river on the lower side, where the old ford can still be seen. The approach to the ford from the east is now covered with the plants of the Common Comfrey (*Symphytum Officinale*). This small area is known locally as Canada, a name, together with Newfoundland, Botany Bay, Van Diemans Land and several others, which was used when the ownership of such land was in question.

Travelling on down the road from the river bridge, in the field on the right is a raised walkway, the old floodpath from the Crosses to the churchyard. There were four wooden gates along the pathway; two are now disused. Each had a floodboard fitted like a small narrow bridge so that it was possible to walk from the main road to the churchyard where high ground could be reached without getting wet. It was just too bad if one of the gates had been left open. This resulted in a soaking. The floodboards, like every other artefact in the parish, now lie neglected or broken.

The B4365 Much Wenlock to Ludlow road was put through in 1863. The Crosses was the old market place, but records of the years when it was functional are not to hand.

The first building on the left moving north was the Crosses Public House, now a double dwelling. This closed as a pub

Previously the Crosses Inn

between 1851 and 1861, either due to the construction of the B4365 or, more likely, due to the departure of the Craven family, and the transferring of the village into fresh hands: the Crosses Public House, the Craven Arms, situated in the centre of the village, together with the Clive Arms at Bromfield, all suffering the same fate. One further house makes up the Crosses, this is situated on the right hand side. Nearby, a stonewall at the roadside is all that remains of the old mill yard of Stanton Lacy watermill.

The Vicarage

Returning to the church, on the right hand side of the road opposite the churchyard is the Vicarage, a fine old building, now private dwellings, with many fine shrubs and trees. One tree in particular one cannot fail to notice is the tall Wellingtonia (*Sequoiadendron giganteum*) that is growing close to the building. Permission was sought to fell this tree, which was thought to be a danger to the building and its occupants, but was refused by the planning authority.

Underneath the trees one may see the plants of the Pink Purslane (*Montia sibirica*). The leaves which were used in salad dishes. There were once 54 acres of glebe land belonging to the Vicarage; these acres are now rented out.

Church of St. Peter, Stanton Lacy

The Churchyard and Cemetery

Both the churchyard and the cemetery consist of made up ground, where the soil has been made up to its present height by the hand of man, so that all the coffins are above, or at, ground level with the road. If we assume that a grave is dug to a depth of 6 ft. it makes one wonder through what the surface water lodged at the roadsides, having seeped through the walls, has passed.

There are many fine old trees in both churchyard and cemetery. Old Corsican Pines (*Pinus Negra*) are home to nesting rooks in spring, bringing sounds and life to this otherwise silent place.

> There's empty acres West and East,
> But yes 'tis gods that grows the least,
> These bountiful acres that they sow,
> With these seeds that will never grow. (*A.E. Housman*)

In the churchyard there is a Wild Service tree (*Sorbus torminalis*). There are now several species of Service tree, mostly hybrids that have been crossed by man, resulting in the *Sorbus torminalis* being known as the 'Wild' variety. I know of just two remote areas of woodland in south Shropshire where this tree does exist in its true wild form, having survived from a parent tree long since disappeared. One of these sites is in Stanton Lacy parish.

In the walls of the church two stone canopied tombs can be seen. Whose remains they contain is anyones guess. The names of 'de lacy' and 'de

The two canopied tombs at St. Peters. Both tombs have stone effigies and underneath are stone coffins

Mortimer' have been put forward, but there are no records of either family having lived, died, or even visited Stanton Lacy, the village not being grand enough to house these Marcher families in life or death.

Many privileged parish families were buried in and close to the church. In those days, if one could afford the fee at all, the more one could afford, the further inside one went. There were no grave stones before the late 16th century. The so called common or poor stock were buried outside in unmarked graves.

Here I lies by the Chancel door,
Here I lies because I'm poor,
The further in the more you pay,
But here lies I, as warm as they. (*Anon.*)

It would be a crime to leave the churchyard of St. Peter without a mention of the snowdrops that form one huge carpet in early spring.

☆ ☆ ☆ ☆

A lane running between the Old Vicarage, Netherhope, and the wall of the cemetery leads to a derelict cottage referred to in years past as the cobbler's shop. Here lived one William Jones, cobbler. William was also Parish Clerk for 51 years. After his death in 1938, his two spinster daughters continued to live in the cottage until the 1960s.

Returning to the road we continue up the village street, passing a black and white house on the right. This was once thatched, and was the residence of the vicar's chauffeur.

Further on on the right are the old school and school house. The school building was built and opened as a school with residence for a schoolmaster in 1872. Arthur Bowskill was its first schoolmaster, he was also postmaster, so one may gather he was a busy man. The building closed as a school in 1982 due to a lack of pupils. A firm specializing in restorations for interior design now occupies the old building. In the old playground, and close to the wall bordering the village street stands a lone Box tree (*Buxus Sempervirens*). There are few of these specimens about, and there should be a preservation order on this tree if there is not one already. Opposite the old school gates a cottage stands on the back drive to Church Farm. This cottage is of a later period than the rest of the street and was probably built around the same time as the school and school house.

Stanton Lacy School in 1939; all classes
Back Row, (left to right): Stella Good, Alice Jones, Ivy Jones, Phylis Davies, Jessie Jones, Irene Davies, Bill Jones
Centre Row: Margaret Maddox, Rosemary Massey, Bob Edwards, Wallace Green, Ivor Good, Martin Good, Muriel Massey, Olive Cornes
Front Row: Richard Green, John Ellams, Philip Downes

Stanton Lacy School in the 1960s; all classes

Further on again lies the Manor House, a building of some considerable age, built on the site of a much older building which may have been the home of the powerful North Herefordshire family of Devereux, who held the Manor of Stanton Lacy under the de Lacys and de Genevilles in the 13th century. The Devereux were said to have lived at Stanton Lacy for a period of time, but many people doubt that this important family could have lived in anything but a fortified manor house or castle at this time in history. The Devereux held five other manors under the de Lacys and de Genevilles at the time they held Stanton Lacy. Sir William Devereux (1230-1265) was a person of some standing, and would have lived in a residence befitting his rank, probably one of his or the de Lacy's Herefordshire castles.

Another black and white cottage stands over the road from the Manor House; this and the next cottage, also black and white, were thatched cottages until the 1950s when the thatch was replaced by shingles of Western Red Cedar.

The black and white cottage nearest the 'T' junction was the wheelwright's shop until the wooden building was built in Carpenters Lane.

The Craven Arms

The house facing us at the 'T' road was once the village pub, The Craven Arms, last recorded as an Inn in the census of 1861, the year before the Cravens left the parish. This building was thatched until the 1950s when it was given a shingle roof like its neighbours. The old pub has been a shop, and post office and shop, during its history. Now it is home to one of the oldest families of the parish, its garden, always a fine picture of flowers and vegetables, making it stand out in the village.

A drive at the side of the Old Post Office takes us up to Manor House Farm, a well built old farmhouse of some considerable age with well laid out gardens.

The Old Post Office, once the Craven Arms

Top: Hay harvest at Manor Farm in 1912

Bottom: Road laying gang at the Manor Farm buildings in the 1920s. Left to right: unknown, Jim Tolley, ? Lewis, Andrew Smout, unknown, unknown, Thomas Clee

The old carpenter's shop

Carpenters Lane runs from the old Craven Arms Inn to the bottom of the Hope, or Hope cross roads. Once a lane of hedged banks full of primroses and violets, it is now nothing but a rutted track, known locally as 'Shit Creek'. On the right hand side of the lane next to a corn drying plant the wooden carpenter's shop is still standing. This shop once employed three people in the carpenter, wheelwright and coffin making business, which was run for many years by the Evison family, Rhesa Evison being the last of the line to practise carpentry here. The home of the Evison family had been the Wheelwrights Cottage already mentioned, the family moving to the old pub, post office in later years, where they were also post-masters or mistresses. After Rhesa Evison's retirement the carpenters shop was changed to an agricultural repair shop with a 'welding plant'. This business was run by Ivor Meredith and the late Derek Hughes. Next to the old carpenters shop and corn drying plant there was a saw pit, where trees were sawn into planks for the carpenter, wheelwright and coffin maker.

There are just two more houses in Carpenters lane, a double dwelling situated on the right hand side.

Blacksmiths Lane

Returning to the Old Post Office, we enter the Blacksmith's Lane. Once another hedged, banked lane with its banks full of wild flowers, adding to the beauty of the village, this lane is now known locally as Tinker's Ally.

Opposite the garden of the old Post Office once stood the village pump. This has now disappeared from sight, but could still be there hidden by under-growth. A small patch of grassed land on the right is the site of the Blacksmith's shop, another of those thatched dwellings bulldozed down in the 1970s to save spending money on their improvement. The shop was circular with a thatched roof. The blacksmith's cottage stood next to the shop, this was

The Forge, now demolished

also thatched. I often watched George Jones, the last blacksmith to practice here, at work at shoeing, or at iron work. The sparks from the hot metal on the anvil fled up into the thatched roof which was tinder dry on the inside and blackened due to millions of sparks which had attempted to burn the thatch, but had failed, the straw being so tightly packed.

The next house on the lane was once a double dwelling, Nos 7 and 8, Blacksmiths Lane. A further 4 houses, 'North Cottages' or the 'Council Houses' built by the council in the 1950s are the last houses on the lane. They are now undergoing renovations, and improvements, which is hoped will bring about a tidying up in general of the whole area.

Blacksmiths Lane runs on to join the Ludlow Peaton road.

☆ ☆ ☆ ☆

Nash's Charity

Richard Nash esq. of Rock Green, Ludlow, by his will dated 15th May 1814, left £100 to the poor of the parish of Stanton Lacy to be placed in the public funds in the names of the minister and churchwardens and the interest thereof to be laid out on bread, to be distributed at their discretion among the poor on Christmas Day.

> It does not appear that this legacy has yet been invested in the public funds, but the annual interest of £5 is annually paid to the parish officers by the bank of Prodgers & Co, at Ludlow, on account of Mr Benjamin Coates of Leominster, one of the executors of Mr Nash's will, and is distributed, in twelvepenny, sixpenny and threepenny loaves, among the poor at Christmas, according to the discretions of the testator.

The above is taken from the Registers of Stanton Lacy parish. If this is a true record, then the twelvepenny loaves must have been of gigantic proportions—I can remember the fourpenny loaf that was with us until 1941, after which it rose to $4\frac{1}{2}$d for a 2lb loaf. I do remember the giving of bread on Christmas Day at Stanton Lacy vicarage, which continued into the 1950s, to then be replaced by the giving of a packet of tea instead. This practice only ceased in recent years.

Poor's Stock

> It is said that this charity was founded in 1639 by various parishioners, partly for the repair of the church, but there appears to be no trust deed of any sort. For some years the income was divided by the trustees between the two schools in the parish viz: the National School and Hayton School, but they appear to have no claim upon it whatever. The stock is now managed by the trustees appointed by the Parish Council, and the income, £2 5s. 8d. is applied to other than educational purposes, and the Board of Education do not claim any authority in the matter.

The above is taken from parish Registers when the Rev. L.R.C. Bagot was vicar. He died in 1922, having become vicar in 1879. An earlier record, from 1819, reads:

> There has been for many years in this parish a fund called the Poor's Stock, which, in the beginning of the present year, 1819, amounted to £40, derived from various and uncertain sources. This fund was left in sums of £5 and £10, in the hands of different persons in the parish, who paid interest for it, which was distributed among the poor, together with the sacrament money, at Easter. In March 1819, £35, part of the stock, together with £1 15s. advanced by the parish, was applied to the purchase of a small house and garden in the Rock Lane, which was conveyed to a trustee for the use of the inhabitants of the parish, to be used as a poor-house; and the parish will continue to pay the interest of the £35, so applied, to be distributed to the poor at Easter as usual. The house is not let, but is used for the reception of paupers.

> The remaining £5 of the Poor's Stock was placed in the hands of John Carter, a farmer in the parish; but he has fallen on hard times, and it is feared the money will be lost. The interest has not been paid by him for a year or two.

The poor-house in Rock Lane would have been lost to the parish when Rock Green was transferred from the parish to that of Ludlow in 1879.

From the parish registers it appears that there was formerly another sum of £10 belonging to the Poor's Stock fund, which came into the hands of one Thomas Norgrove, farmer and churchwarden. After his death, which occurred around 1784, it disappears from the account, and is supposed to be lost. Yet a further, undated, entry reads:

> It appears from the books of the parish, which were produced before us, that a sum of £12, described as 'The full Poor's Stock', was, in the year 1758, returned by Francis Hudson into the hands of John Acton then one of the parish officers; and that, in the year 1762, when Francis Hudson came into office as overseer of the poor, he received it back from Acton. We find no further mention of this money in the books; but it is ascertained to have been in the hands of Hudson at the time of his death, and for several years before and that he annually paid the interest, which was added to the sacrament money, and distributed among the poor of the parish. After his death, his son Francis (who was appointed co-executor with his brother Edward) continued to pay the interest until his death, which took place about 1806, since which time in consequence, as it appears, of a misunderstanding, no payment has been made. This misunderstanding, however, has been happily removed, and Mrs Hudson, the widow and executrix of Francis Hudson the younger, has expressed her readiness to pay all arrears of interest, together with the principal.

The records conclude:

> We have been unable to procure any satisfactory information as to the real origin of this 'Poor's Stock', but there is a tradition in the parish, that it was part of a sum of £40, which was left by some unknown benefactor, the interest to be paid to the poor; that it finally came into the hands of a person of the name of Higgins, who became insolvent, and the sum of £12 was all that could be recovered.

It may have been from the interest of this remaining £12, that bread was still being distributed on Christmas Day during my boyhood!

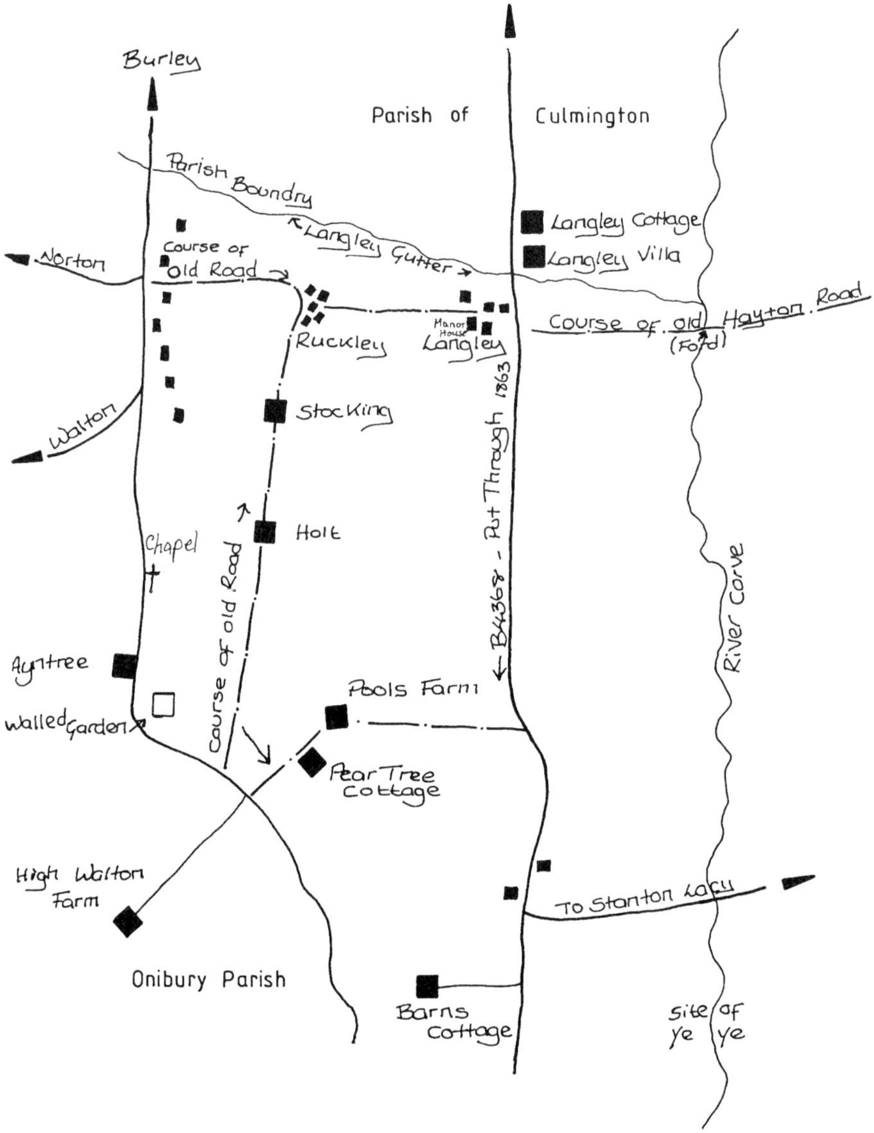

Map of Langley, Ruckley, Stocking and Holt

CHAPTER V

Langley, Ruckley, Stocking & Holt

Langley

Langley from the Old English *Long-lea*, a name given to a long field or wood, is now, and has been for many, many, years, a large mixed farm that has remained in the same family for several generations. Langley Manor House is a 16th century listed building in black and white. In my opinion it is the gem of the parish where buildings are concerned. It is a great pity that the two modern houses were built between the road and the Manor, for these two well kept properties have taken some of the romance from this fine old building. Near to the Manor House old platforms can be traced. These are no doubt the remains of the old settlement that accompanied the Manor, but made out of inferior materials to those of the Manor House, they quickly fell into disrepair. I can find no true record of the 'township of Langley'. The Parish of Stanton Lacy ends a little further up the road, where it joins the Parish of Culmington, Langley gutter forming the Parish boundaries.

Ruckley

Ruckley, from the Old English for 'Rook Lea' or 'ley', a place frequented by rooks, either to feed, or roost, was once an independent farm but is now farmed from one of the neighbouring farms. Old platforms are in evidence together with traces of ridge and furrow.

Stocking

Stocking, again Old English, for land that had been cleared of timber to create farmland. The resulting stumps from the timber were 'stocked' around with mattocks, (a tool resembling a pickaxe, but with a 2" wide cutter on one side of the head and a 4" wide spade head on the other side), then pulled out by horse power. This must have been hard, brutal work for both man and horse.

Holt

Holt, is another Old English place name meaning at the wood, or thicket. This farmstead, like Stocking and Ruckley, is no longer an individual farm, but is farmed within a larger unit. The houses as they were, have disappeared. Traces of platforms can be traced, but it is difficult to say if these are old house platforms, or just the foundations of old farm buildings. The traces of banks at Langley, Ruckley, Stocking and Holt, may be traces of old dwellings, or just where field boundaries have been taken out to form larger fields, but all four areas show banks and ridges on aerial photographs.

Vernolds Common

Vernolds, a mis-spelling of Fernolds, is an Old English name given to a field or area where ferns grow. Vernolds Common is one of those areas that appears not to belong to Stanton Lacy parish, when in fact part of it does. Pools Farm, together with several cottages—Yew Tree Cottage, The Thatches, Keepers Cottage, The Curlews, and Nos.2, 4 and 5, Vernolds Common—belong in Stanton Lacy. The Wesleyan Chapel (recently sold and now a private dwelling) and Ayntree, (Old English, 'place of the lone tree'), are also in the parish of Stanton Lacy.

Below Ayntree there remains Barns Cottage, situated between the B4365 and Ayntree road, and several cottages around Ludlow Racecourse. This ends Stanton Lacy Parish to the South.

YeYe

YeYe was said to have been a 'township' in the Parish of Stanton Lacy, situated at OS 495783, that is today on the left hand side of the road from the Crosses to the Racecourse, near the River Corve. YeYe is a strange name for an old village. It was last recorded in 1350 as derelict and waste. Most old villages within south Shropshire differ only by a letter or so from the 'New Villages' that were built to replace them, but there is no trace of YeYe from the ground level, or from the air. I found this most interesting and puzzling, until I looked back through history to Saxon times, where I found YeYe was the Saxon term for a 'swine pasture'. Perhaps YeYe was no more than an enclosure for swine, with a few crude huts to house swine and swineherd. The absence of any sign of a settlement from the air would support this theory.

CHAPTER VI

The Peaton to Ludlow Toll Road

From the parish boundary near where the Hope brook runs underneath the Ludlow Peaton road, heading towards Lower Hayton, you pass on the right the spot where the old drovers road entered the 'lower toll road'—it is still plainly visible. The woods that run along the ridge to our right are called collectively Stanton Lacy Woods; individually they are Hopes Plantation, Vicarage Wood, Rotting Wood, Palmers Wood and Titterhill Wood. These woods are full of old charcoal hearths, pits from whence limestone has been dug, small building stone quarries, and one small sawpit, now all but filled in and unnoticeable.

A sawpit operated in the following way. The pit was dug just deep enough to take the length of saw to be used. Trees were rolled onto a framework built over the pit and were sawn longways into planks with the pitsaw. The foreman, or head woodman, stood on top of the framework to pull the heavy saw up, the boy or the underwoodman stood in the bottom of the pit pulling the saw down on its cutting stroke. The saw only cut on the downward stroke, meaning that the person in the pit received all the sawdust, or anything else that was falling. It was from the practice of pitsawing that the term 'top dog' and 'under dog' derived. In the 1930s an old pitsaw lay by the side of the pit, but this heavy implement of torture, as it was known to its users, disappeared during the war, no doubt taken as scrap iron to help the war effort.

Passing the entrance to Blacksmiths Lane on the left you cross over a hump in the road where it passes over a ridge of limestone. This has been known for generations as the Bran-dash. It is in fact the Brand-Ash, and refers to the fields, not the road. The name Brand-Ash can be found in many areas

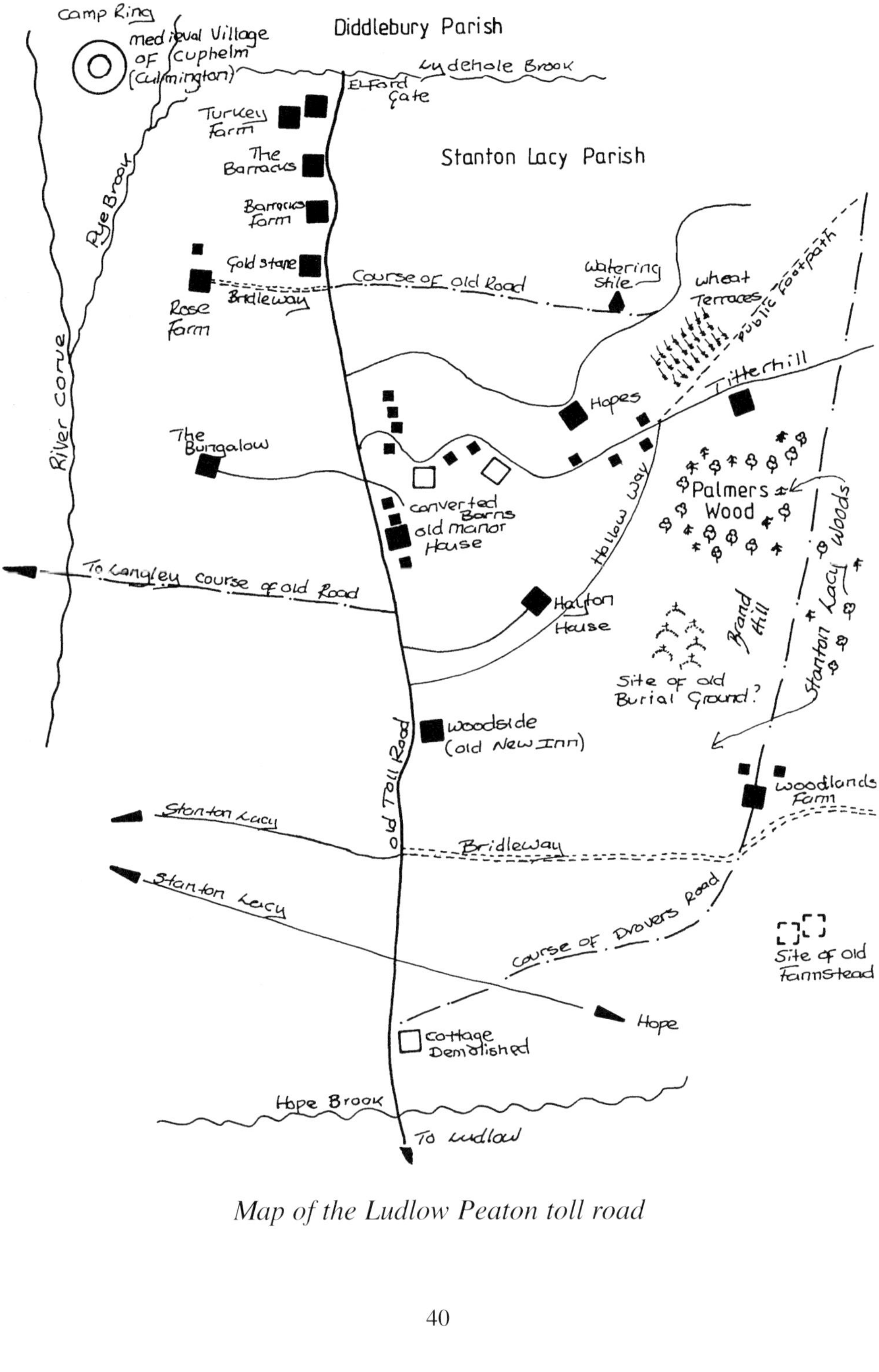

Map of the Ludlow Peaton toll road

of the country, and was used to describe an area of land that had been cleared by fire—*i.e.* the firebrand, a rush torch soaked in pitch, and the resulting ash. Above the wood at this point lies Brandhill, referring to another area that was cleared by use of the firebrand.

On the right, some 200 metres from the Brand Ash, a small circle of Blackthorn can be seen in the field. This surrounds the spring from whence the occupants of the Yeld Farm obtained their drinking water. This spring never runs dry, even during the very dry summers of 1947, '75, '76, '95 and '96, it babbled merrily on.

The Yeld Farm, its name derived from the Old English 'helde'—a slope, a holding of some 50 acres (20 hectares), once covered the area from the well to the wood above and all that land to the right of the present road to the New Inn. The farmhouse and buildings stood on the slope above the well, where now only a lone oak tree stands, their remains being demolished in the 1950s. The Yeld Farm has been farmed from Manor Farm, Stanton Lacy since the 1920s.

The next house on the right is Woodside, quite a large house, which was until February, 1957, the local pub, the New Inn—now a private modernised dwelling.

The 'New Inn', Hayton

The New Inn was built as an inn in 1819 and opened in 1820, closing its doors for the last time on 11th February, 1957. The original building consisted of two kitchens, a parlour, 5 bedrooms, plus stabling for two horses. It had been built as a public house to cater for the increase in traffic and travellers along the greatly improved 'Toll Road' to Ludlow. These road improvements were due to the coming of the railways for stock could now be driven with ease along these improved roads to the railway sidings, from whence they could be transported by rail to their distant destinations in a short time. The journey had taken drovers, using the drovers' roads, days, or even weeks!

Woodside, once the New Inn

The nature of trade of the New Inn was listed in the parish constable's annual report as being 'Agricultural and Roadside', but in 1901 it had changed to 'Mining, Agricultural and Roadside'. This was during a further unsuccessful attempt to find copper ore at Hayton.

Under age drinking appears to have been a problem of longstanding. From the New Inn's records we gather that on May 29th, 1882, the landlord was fined 20/- and 12/6d costs for supplying liquors to children under 16 years of age. The same landlord was fined 10/6d with 17/- costs on 3rd May, 1897 for the selling of adulterated gin.

In the beer garden at the New Inn in the 1920s. On the left is Ernest Edwards, the Rev. R.R. Armitage's chauffeur, central is Thomas Smout with mine host, Mrs. Price, on the right

In the mid-1950s the New Inn was modernised and the archway which had formed the access into the cobbled yard was demolished, together with the stables. Another wing was added, and a piece of land was purchased by the brewery to build a car park and toilet block, but unfortunately the pub closed the following year, much to the disgust of most people of the parish.

Before they were demolished, and as late as the 1950s, the stables had been in use for many activities. Many customers had spent a night in the stable after having a gutfull. Card schools were held between lunchtime closing and evening opening times at weekends, gallon jars of beer were purchased during opening hours and carried out in preparation. Pitch and Toss, and Crown and

Anchor were played in the yard. Disputes were also settled in the yard, one to one being the rule; none of this cowardly one against a gang like today.

Nigel, the dentist from Craven Arms, arrived on a motorcycle about once a month, and after a couple of scotches, would draw teeth in the stable, many of the farmworkers being too scared to normally visit a dentist, or just not having the time.

Ern Wilde, from Hopton Gate, always carried his hair cutting clippers with him on his Sunday lunchtime visits, and would cut hair in the stable, having first slackened his thirst. Although all these activities must have been illegal on licensed premises, all continued until the 1950s. The stables also acted as changing rooms for Hayton and Stan United Football team, formed in 1947 to play in the South Shropshire League. Wearing a black and white strip, they were known as the Magpies. After match baths were taken in two small zinc baths situated in the stables—a couple of buckets of hot water from the pub were emptied into each bath, mixed with a couple of buckets of cold from the pump in the yard, and 22 men would attempt to clean themselves of

Hayton & Stan United Football Team, 1950
Back Row: (left to right): The late Ted Lewis, the late Bert Bagley, the late Jack Tolley, Eric Price, the late Gordon Minton, Bill Jones
Front Row: Harold Rawlings, Dennis Richards, Harold Edwards, the late Dennis Wilcox, Gerald Price, Frank Penny

the clinging red clay. Disputes between players which had started during the match were often settled in the stables at bath time.

Hayton and Stan's pitch was on the field farmed from the Woodlands Farm, their only field to border onto the Ludlow Peaton road.

The team was disbanded in 1955. During their eight years in the South Shropshire League, the team had given much entertainment to those who supported them. The team was fit if nothing else, prepared to chase every ball out of position and control and they raced about the pitch in all directions—just like a litter of pigs on being given their freedom for the first time.

Leaving Woodside, we travel on along the Ludlow Peaton road to Lower Hayton; Nether Hayton or Hayton Inferior as it was known in the 13th century. Hayton, is a Saxon name for a clearing within the wood, or a small managed park within the forest.

On the right is a drive that takes us up to Hayton House, a drive which is in fact the mouth of the old hollowway that was the only road up to Top Titterhill and Hayton Bent before the mid-18th century.

CHAPTER VII

Lower Hayton & 'Nuns Yard'

Lower Hayton was once a township in its own right, having a manor, known in the 13th century as Hayton Inferior or Nether Hayton. The manor was probably under the wing of Stanton Lacy, but the Tyrel family, who held it in the 13th century also owned some of the land outright, as we shall later gather.

In the 1841 census Lower Hayton consisted of 535 acres of land, 24 houses and 104 inhabitants, the principal landowner being the Earls of Craven who subsequently sold the land in 1862.

If we discount the barn conversions, we shall see how Lower Hayton's population has shrunk in 150 years. There are now just 9 houses standing that were probably standing in 1841—New Inn (Woodside), Hayton House, The White House (Hayton Grange), Orchard House, The Glebe, Spring Bank, Rose Farm, North Cottage (Goldstone) and Barracks Farm.

The other houses have been demolished or fallen down over the years since the survey—The Yeld in the 1950s, Nos.1, 2 and 3, Peewit Hall, in the 1960s or 70s, Halls Cottage, situated off Titterhill Lane, just above Glebe Cottage. The entrance to this dwelling can be seen with the ditch piped at this spot, the remains of this dwelling finally disappearing in the 1960s. On up Titterhill Lane, the baking oven of another dwelling still stands proudly at the roadside. Until the practice of bulldozing out fields and orchards, house platforms were to be found at Lower Hayton. Many of these were remains of the Nether Hayton or Hayton Inferior of the 13th century, when the township was made up of more than 30 dwellings, but more of this later.

Of the remaining houses, the first house after the New Inn is Hayton House, a large stone building with a small farm now attached, but Hayton House once had much more land than it does today.

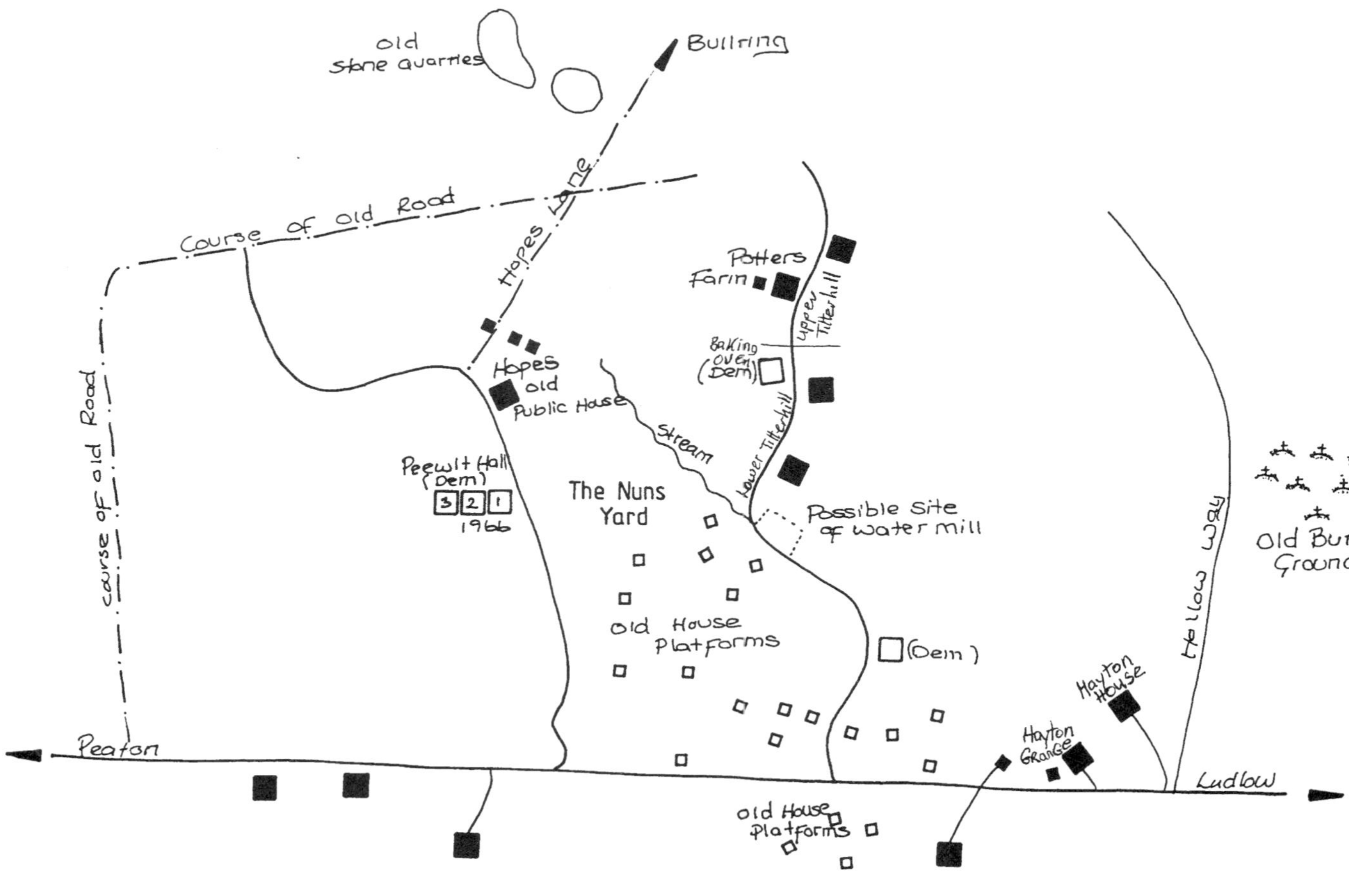

Map of Lower Hayton and Nuns Yard

The next house is now called Hayton Grange, once the White House: a pair of wrought iron gates set in a pink coloured brick wall form the entrance but look out of place, much like a brass knob on an earthen privy door would look. But still, what is one man's meat is another man's poison!

Close to Hayton House and Hayton Grange, was situated the Manor House of the Tyrel family. This family was holding part of Nether Hayton in 1260 under the Genevilles and de Lacys, but the Tyrel family also owned lands in Nether Hayton independent of the de Lacy Manor.

Barn conversions have been made around the old White House, making comfortable homes out of once redundant barns. In the gable end of the last barn conversion to touch the road, the Royal Mail collection box was set into the wall of the old barn. In the walls of this same barn, 50 or 60 years ago, there was a loose stone with a cavity behind it, where pipe smoking men left their 'scorks' for Black Jack Matthews to collect. 'Scorks' are the remains of a pipe decoke. Old pipe smokers would periodically decoke their pipes, leaving the scorks, with any 'baccy' they considered to be too dry to smoke in this wall cavity for Jack, who would chew this wet mess. Black Jack hated all boys and would chase them on sight, so to even things up we mixed horse muck with his scorks, replacing the mess in the wall for Jack to collect and chew. Perhaps he in turn chased us to even things up in his opinion. Had silage been about in those days Jack may have acquired a taste for it. I have no doubt that the opportunity for him to do so would have arisen.

Ted Bridgewater, the local rabbit catcher

On the opposite side of the road to the White House and Hayton Grange, a bungalow can be seen in the field. This was built in the 1960s, and is the only attempt this century at building on the lower side of the road from the parish boundary at Hope Brook. There is no fall for drainage, so very few attempts have been made at building on this lower side.

Lower Titterhill Lane is then reached. The first house in the lane is Orchard House, a stone and brick affair with a modern extension to the rear.

A community well is situated opposite Orchard House, where everyone drew their water supply during dry summers. Even the occupants of Peewit Hall carried their drinking water from here.

Glebe Cottage, just above the well, is now a dwelling of some considerable size, with tidily laid out gardens, a far cry from the small overgrown building of the 1970s. We will return to Glebe Cottage later.

Moving on up the lane we arrive at Spring Bank Cottage, once a lovely sunny place with a wealth of snowdrops, followed by banks of primroses and violets. It is hoped that the new owners will return the dwelling and gardens to their past glory in the near future!

Above Spring Bank a 1960s bungalow has been built on the right hand side of the lane with tidily laid out gardens adjoining. The area above this bungalow is classed as being in Upper Hayton.

Glebe Cottage. It was connected to the Nuns Yard, after which it became Glebe land to the Church

In the fields above Lower Hayton, around OS 506805, there is reputed to be an ancient burial ground—but I am unable to find any record to support this. It may be that something has been picked out on an aerial photograph, but nothing has been proven.

Returning to the bottom road, if you take the right hand fork to Upper Hayton, there is a finger post erected in 1995 pointing to Upper Hayton and Haytons Bent. Before, the old finger post pointed to Upper Hayton and Hayton Bent, the last post left in the parish to give the hamlet of Hayton Bent its correct name. (Hayton derives from the town in the clearing in the wood, whilst Bent is the Saxon term for a grassy slope. Now it is Hayton's Bent, the letter 's' having been added by those immigrants who obviously do not know the meaning of the word Hayton or Bent; this of course includes Shropshire County Council. We now see a barn conversion in black and white, with a garage to match. This dwelling, together with a further cottage, have been constructed out of the old Glebe Farm buildings.

Travelling on, you reach a small enclosure on the left hand side of the road, now filled with straw bales and farm machinery. This was the site of three cottages, 1, 2 and 3, Peewit Hall, which were demolished in the late 1960s. Along the field on the left hand side there existed another 'watering stile' and a hem-wall (a wall to 'hem' or enclose), which might suggest that there was an enclosure here for stock. An old trackway once existed connecting Upper Hayton and the Ludlow Peaton road along this line.

Opposite to Peewit Hall, the area is known as the Nuns Yard. Much has been made of this name over the years. The main line of thought has been that there once existed a holy house of some description here under the wing of Wenlock Abbey. Nothing could be further from the truth, which we will see in a Chapter on Nuns Yard!

The last house that I consider to be included in Lower Hayton, (there are no set boundaries, except for postal reasons), is Hopes Farm House, an old house built in stone with an extension in brick, which one will notice was not tied into the original building and now shows a slight tendency to slip. The Hopes was once a Public House and farm. It closed as a public house during the 1850s, since being run as a farm

Hopes Farm, once a public house

Farmers' Corner outside the Hopes

only. The corner in the road outside the Hopes is known as 'Farmers' Corner', and is said to have been a place where local farmers met for a chat.

A lane ran up from the Hopes to the Bullring, through Balcony Orchard, up the side of Balcony Bank, through Balcony Close to Balcony Cottage, (now called Dale View Cottage); but we will deal with the Bullring in a separate chapter.

Returning to the Ludlow Peaton road and turning right, some 300 metres up the road is a lane to the left. This was once the lane to Rose Farm. It once ran across the present road to the 'watering stile' and close to the hem-wall, then on to Upper Hayton. Rose Farm is now a private dwelling, stripped of its small farm. Again we notice that it is one of those few dwellings that have been erected on the lower side of the road. All the land from Rose Farm to and around Stanton Lacy, was, until the 1970s, prime beef producing water meadows, with an occasional corn field in between. Now, hedges have been taken out, and large cornfields have been made at the taxpayers' expense.

We now return to the road and continue on. The next dwelling, also on the left is Goldstone, once North Cottage. The house was once a butcher's shop run by Thomas Bengry, later a dairy farm run by William Henner, who many people of the parish will remember living at No.2 Hayton Bent in later years. Goldstone has now been modernised without spoiling its old character.

The next house on the left is Barracks Farm, another small farm of some 30 acres, (12.3 ha), which belonged to the Tanner family. Again the farmland has been taken off the house.

Beyond are the last two houses in the parish, a double dwelling once belonging to the same Tanner family. Mr. William Tanner had the dwellings built in the early years of the present century naming them Russelldene and Marydene, after Russell and Mary, his son and daughter.

Just beyond these two cottages, huge turkey sheds stand on the left hand side. Within these, thousands of turkeys are reared for the meat trade. Our journey ends at Elford gate, where the brook runs underneath the road and where once there was a ford, with a boundary gate. 'Elford' is either derived from the ford in the elder grove, or the ford of the eels; both interpretations can be found listed—but I prefer the former, right or wrong!

Baugh's 1808 map shows a cott near here, but there are no signs of any remains. Maybe it stood where Russelldene and Marydene now stand, and was demolished for that purpose.

Moving away from the road at this point, in a westerly direction, we travel over the fields to the Pyebrook. Across the Pyebrook, and situated between it and the River Corve, is an old earthwork called Camp Ring which, from evidence on the ground and from aerial photography, one can plainly see has been an old settlement, with a Motte and Bailey. Erosion and ploughing is now taking its toll of this mediaeval village. Camp Ring is certainly not its correct name; research has resulted in my thinking that this is the site of the old Culmington Village (*Cuphelm-ton*, Old English, the tun-of-Cuphelm's people).

Mr. and Mrs. Hotchkiss with Eddie, their son, in between, with Grace and Bobbie James, evacuees from Liverpool, in 1939

We now end our journey through this part of Stanton Lacy Parish and return to Upper Hayton.

The Nuns Yard

There has existed at Lower Hayton for many years a puzzle concerning an area called 'The Nuns Yard'. I myself had given very little thought to the origins of the name before I began my research. It was during this research, that I became aware of the truth concerning The Nuns Yard. We must travel back through history to the year 1260 to begin to get a true picture.

The records state that Sir William Devereux, his wife Matilda and their young son, (also William), members of the powerful north Herefordshire family of that name, were holding the vill of Hayton Inferior together with seven other manors under the de Genevilles. Sir William and Matilda drew 24 merks of rent from the township of Nether Hayton, that is to say that they received the rents from 24 properties, making one realize how large Lower Hayton was in those days. They had also purchased from Sir Roger Tyler two merks of rent. It can be supposed that they now held these two properties outright.

Sir William Devereux fell on the rebel side in the battle of Evesham, 1265. The church would have, in normal circumstances, punished Matilda and her son William for Sir William's treachery. Maybe the fact that Walter Giffard, Bishop of Bath and Wells, who would have been responsible for Matilda's punishment, was her brother helped to enable Matilda and son to keep their lands.

In 1285, William Devereux II was holding part of Nether Hayton under Peter de Geneville. Matilda had remarried to one Walter de La Barre and had been granted five acres of meadow land and one water mill in Nether Hayton, together with the 24 merks of rent. These were all to be held by Matilda and Walter and their heirs during their lifetime. But by the year 1282, Walter Giffard had been followed by Robert Burnell as bishop. He possessed a long memory and bloodstained grabbing hands, which was then typical of members of the church. From a fine levied at Westminster on October 6th 1285:

> Bishop Robert Burnell, Plaintiff, sued William Devereux II for 24 merks of rent, five acres of meadow land and one watermill in the Ville of Hayton inferior held now by the said Matilda and Walter de La Barre and William Devereux, shall go to the Bishop and his heirs after the deaths of the said Walter and Matilda de La Barre, when such reversion would otherwise pertain to the said William Devereux. The Bishop is to hold the whole at one penny rent under William Devereux and his heirs.

Matilda and Walter de La Barre came to court and swore that they did not oppose the ruling. William Devereux also signed. The Bishop paid one sparrowhawk for the grant. Witnesses were Sir Roger Tyler of Heyton, 'knight', Sir Roger de Baskerville of Lawton, 'knight', William de Clifford of Corfham, Master Richard Heyton and Master William Andreu. Elias de Sutton of Sutton was held responsible to see that the ruling was carried out in all departments. This was a case of daylight robbery by the Church, who as I have said before, were, in those days, capable of anything.

Matilda still held her two merks of rent on the land she owned. These were:

£1. 2. 0d	on a Virgate held by William Hauman* and
4. 8d	on the tenement of Richard fitz Robert
Total £1. 6. 8d	

In 1289 Matilda made a gift of these rents to the 'Prioress and Nuns of the Convent of Aconbury', which lies south of Hereford (OS 506332). Kathleen de Lacy was prioress at the time. The gift was given and received, showing once again how Stanton Lacy was tied to the County of Herefordshire by the de Lacys. These two merks of rent gifted to the nuns of Aconbury Priory were drawn from that area of Nether Hayton or Lower Hayton that have been known since as the Nuns Yard!! Elias de Sutton was once again engaged to see that all was legally carried out.

Many claims and counter claims appear to have been made concerning these two merks of rent, but they were still being paid to the convent at the time of the destruction of the priory by Henry VIII. After, they were claimed by the Church as Glebe, hence Glebe Cottage. We find around the Nuns Yard several fields called Church Furlong, recalling that he old field systems were laid out in furlong strips. The greedy grasping Church, usually had several strips within the system. Here I will add a note of caution: one must not get the Church Furlongs and those fields marked Churchmans mixed up; Churchman fields were those fields owned by the powerful Churchman family who lived in the neighbouring parishes of Diddlebury and Munslow. It seems to have been a practice to have a little land in neighbouring parishes, probably through purchase or marriage, which could provide a stepping stone to other things.

---

*Haumon, Heyton, Heytone, Haemon, Heymon are all misspellings (or old spellings) of Hayton.

Hereford steers in the 1920s, now a rare sight

CHAPTER VIII

Over Hayton : Upper Hayton

Leaving the Hopes we now arrive at Upper Hayton. The term Lower and Upper do not appear to have been used before the 18th Century, Nether and Over being the norm.

The first house on the left hand side of the road is the White House which was once the Manor House of the township of Upper Hayton. It is obviously a building of some considerable age, but incorporates the remains of a much older building than even the outside suggests. It appears from the inside that stabling may also have been incorporated into the main building at some stage in its history.

The next building is situated a little further up the road, up a short drive on the right hand side. This is the Mansion House, previously the Manor House, a black and white listed building built by the Craven family around 1625! In 1624 Elizabeth, widow of Sir Richard Craven, purchased the Manor of Stanton Lacy from the Crown. The Craven family held the manor and were patrons of the living until most of the parish of Stanton Lacy was sold off in lots in 1862. Door hinges both in the house and some of the outbuildings bear the crest and name of the Craven family. The Mansion House and the White House are now private dwellings with small farms attached.

From the census of 1841 we gather that the hamlet of Upper Hayton together with Hayton Bent consisted of 935 acres of land, 56 houses with 256 inhabitants.

A small cottage in an orchard on the left hand side of the road at its junction with Mulberry Lane is named Mulberry Cottage. There do not appear to be any records, or any sign of there ever being any mulberry trees planted or

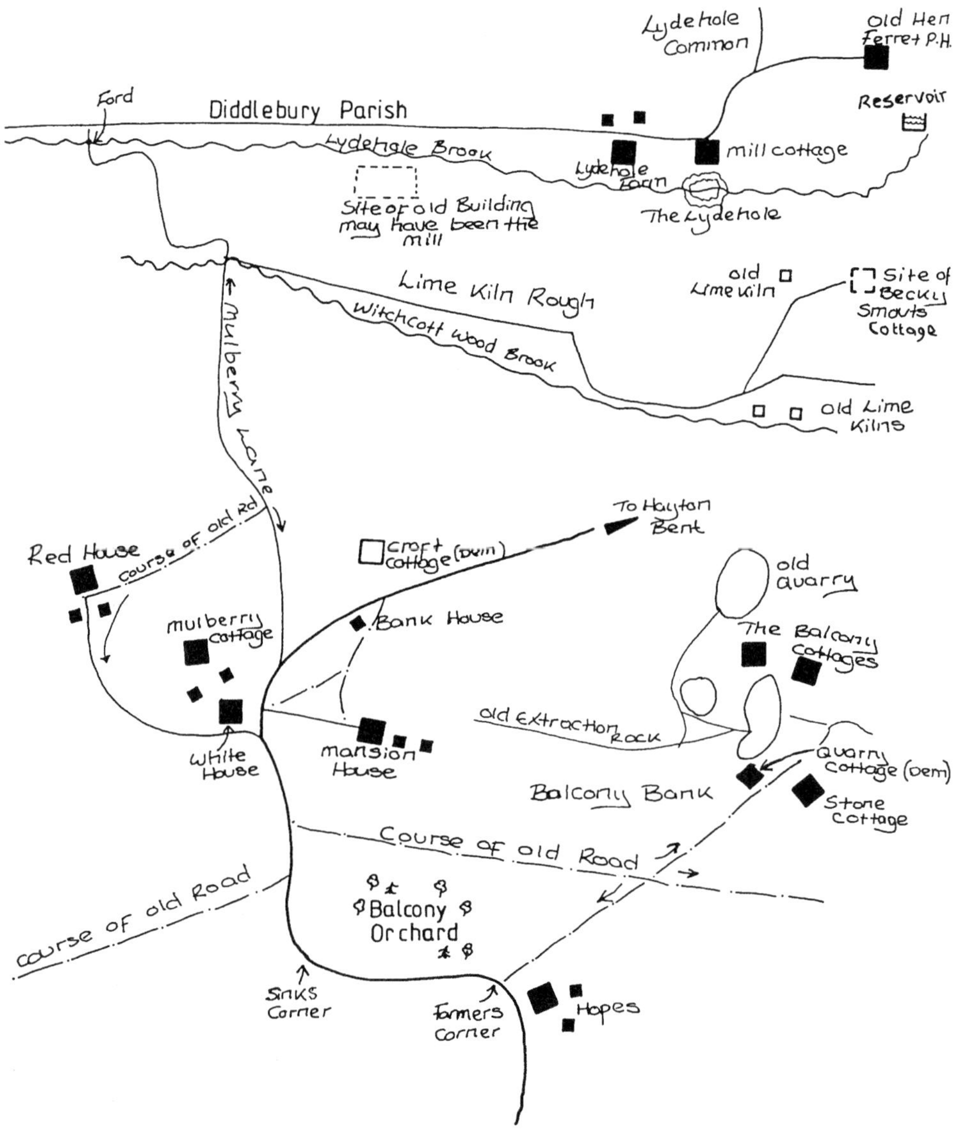

Map of Upper Hayton

Two views of The Mansion House

grown here, and the name probably derives from the East Anglian term by which the bramble bush is known. The bramble is also the mulberry bush in the children's nursery rhyme 'Here we go round the Mulberry bush', the berries of the bramble looking very similar to the berries of the Mulberry tree. Mulberry Cottage is a charming little building ripe for renovation, which I fear would spoil its old world charm. The property has been empty and derelict for many years.

Mulberry Lane

Mulberry Lane leads from the bottom of Hayton Bank to Lydehole Farm, and thus out of the parish of Stanton Lacy.

On the right hand side of the lane, some 70 metres from its junction with Hayton Bank, we can see the old mine workings where the William Lovett Mining Company tried unsuccessfully to find enough copper ore to satisfy the overlords in the 1850s.

Further along the lane on the left hand side is Red House Farm, a red brick building, which is most uncommon in this part of the parish. The Red House dates from the early part of the 19th century and is now the last house standing along Mulberry Lane.

The land begins to change at this point. On the left hand side the land is reasonably flat; on the right hand side the fields become smaller leading up to rough land and scrub woodland named Arbour Hill, now the home of hundreds of rooks and jackdaws that nightly gather here to roost. This land was once farmed and the old field hedgerows can still be plainly seen. Much of the land was grazed until the 1940s, but scrub has now covered the whole area, turning it back to rough woodland.

Mulberry Lane passes over a piped stream, Witchcot Brook, where there was a ford until some 50 years ago. Across the brook, a gate with a roadway leads up to Lime Kiln Rough, a wood planted by the Forestry Commission in 1958-59. But up until the first half of the present century, this area was thriving. Hurdle making, lime stone burning and charcoal burning were carried out here, all vital to the rural community and economy. The making of charcoal only ceased in 1952.

Charcoal

Many charcoal hearths can be found within Lime Kiln Rough, Trenchers Wood, Passeys Wood and Witchcot Wood, the four areas of woodland that now make up this one block. The traditional way of making charcoal had been practised here for many years, but during the 1940s and until production ceased in 1952, the round drum method was in use. The old method of making charcoal was to cover the materials with earth. The drum method cut out this long and lengthy practice of earthing over, the wood and fire being covered by a metal drum, similar to a funnel turned upside down, which fitted on a framework positioned above the stack. Only one man was needed to work a plant once the drum method had been introduced.

As lads in the early 1940s we were commissioned by Albert, then the lone burner, to try to find him spindleberry wood, which makes the finest charcoal. This strong slim charcoal went to make artists' pencils and was the perk of the burner, as he sold it on the side to make a little extra cash. Most farmers were glad to have the spindleberry tree cut from their land as long as hedges were not destroyed in the process, for they are the overwintering host for the bean aphid. By removing the spindleberry, we were doing a service to both the farmer and the charcoal burner. Seeing that the spindleberry will only grow on limestone, numbers were never very great and wages for our services were accordingly low. We did not make our fortunes!

Limeburning

Limestone must have once been a great asset to the rural community. Trenching and burning were carried out in this part of the parish into the early years of the present century. Two stone hearths remain *in situ* along the sides of the brook in Lime Kiln Rough and Witchcot Wood, whilst a third built of brick lies on the hillside close to the remains of Becky Smout's Cottage. Trenches from which the limestone was dug are everywhere within the wood. To distinguish the burners from the diggers, they were termed 'burner' and 'trencher', the burner being considered to be the more important, therefore entitled to higher wages. The trenching was considered to need less skill (anyone can dig), and the trencher therefore received a lower wage. Trenchers Wood got its name from these limestone workers.

Hurdle Making

Hurdle making in Witchcot Wood ceased in the very early years of the 20th century, but in my youth many of the older men then living could remember the hurdlemaker. Hurdles were made from Hazel wands, the Hazel bushes being coppiced every seven years.

Witchcot Wood

The name Witchcot was given to the whole block of this woodland by the Forestry Commission when they leased the property from the Church Commissioners in 1950. The present crop was planted in 1958 and 1959, and consists of Japanese, hybrid and European larch, Norway spruce, western red cedar interplanted with oak and beech. A small experimental patch of tulip trees (*Liriodendron tullipifera*) was planted by me on behalf of the Forestry Commission close to the Lydehole Brook in 1959. Unfortunately this plot was destroyed by grey squirrels which stripped off the bark to reach the sugary sap underneath.

The Boyne Estates, who had purchased the Peaton Estate from the Church Commissioners in the 1960s, was given lease back from the Forestry Commission in the mid 1980s.

Becky Smout

Very little remains of Becky Smout's Cottage which was situated on the slopes above the small field that is now more or less surrounded by the wood. The house platform and remains of the hedge which enclosed the property can be picked out. Becky was a witch according to local people, being deformed, and therefore shunned by most. She was obviously ripe for ridicule and blame in the mid-19th century and in around 1850 Becky fled to live with her sister on Silvington Common (OS 622792), but a bad name travels fast! A year or two later Becky had moved to a remote hamlet in the hills around Clun. What treatment she received here is unknown, but 50 years later, when she must have been a great age, we find that she was once again accused of witchcraft, this in 1898. She was accused of 'overlooking' (putting a curse upon someone or something) a local man and his family over a quarrel concerning chicken corn. Their chickens died, whilst the man and his family became ill with no interest in living. The medical men were brought in, but could find nothing wrong with the family except their insistence that they had been overlooked, and were therefore doomed. Many of the older people in the area falsely swore in front of the authorities that Becky was a witch, and that they had seen her arriving on a broomstick some 50 years ago from Silvington on Clee Hill side. Seeing that this happened at the turn of the present century, we can only imagine that the whole matter was laughed off, but the end of this episode is unknown, and what happened to my great, great Aunt Becky is a mystery. (See Lady Catherine Mills Gasskell's *Spring in a Shropshire Abbey* for a full report on the Clun incident)

The Lydehole

Returning to Mulberry Lane and continuing along towards the Lydehole Brook which runs in a ford over the road and forms the boundary between the parishes of Stanton Lacy and Diddlebury, a recent drive to Mill Cottage runs away to the right. A house once stood on the left of the drive close to the brook, but was demolished in the late 1940s. Mill Cottage and Lydehole Farmhouse stand in Diddlebury Parish, but Lydehole itself is part of the parish boundary.

A Lyde or Lye was a name given to a deep hole formed by running water and to which wood ash was added to make the water more alkaline, hemp and flax being stiffened and whitened in this way. However this Lydehole was a natural Lye. The parish records refer to Lydehole brook thus:

> A small rivulet which flows from the hilly ground becomes on its passage through the rocks strongly impregnated with carbonate of lime, and is found to possess the property of forming petrifactions of such articles as are placed in it.

I can find no evidence of a mill ever having stood at the Lydehole, despite a Mill Cottage. Rocque's map of 1752 and Baugh's map of 1808 make no mention of there being a mill here. Considering that the Mill Cottage is not a building of any great age, one can only ponder.

The house that was demolished in 1940 and which stood close to Mulberry Lane may have been the mill, and also may have been the home of the following, as detailed in the Parish Records:

> Elianor ap David and Mary ap David, daughters of Margaret ap David widow of Lyde Hole found guilty of stealing one goose from the Common, property of one Thomas Garbett, the said Thomas Garbett and the Constable are to place them in the stocks for one whole day with the goose there.

If we consider that the brook has formed the parish boundary from the time that the parishes were marked out, had the Davids lived at the present Lyde Hole Farm they would have been dealt with by the Court of Diddlebury Parish, not Stanton Lacy.

A man or woman,
Must be a wrong un,
To steal a goose
From off the Common,
But the man's without excuse
Who stole the Common
From the goose (*Anon.*)

☆ ☆ ☆ ☆

Mulberry Lane formed part of the old drovers' road and packhorse lane system that can be traced throughout Shropshire. From the parish boundary at Lydehole Brook the old way ran over Lydehole Common to Sutton Hill, a hamlet in the parish of Diddlebury. The old public house along the drovers road, The Hen and Ferret is still standing. The building was sold in the 1980s, but sadly the name of the old pub had changed when advertised for sale and had become The Hen and Pheasant—but now I am poaching in Diddlebury Parish, and must return to Stanton Lacy.

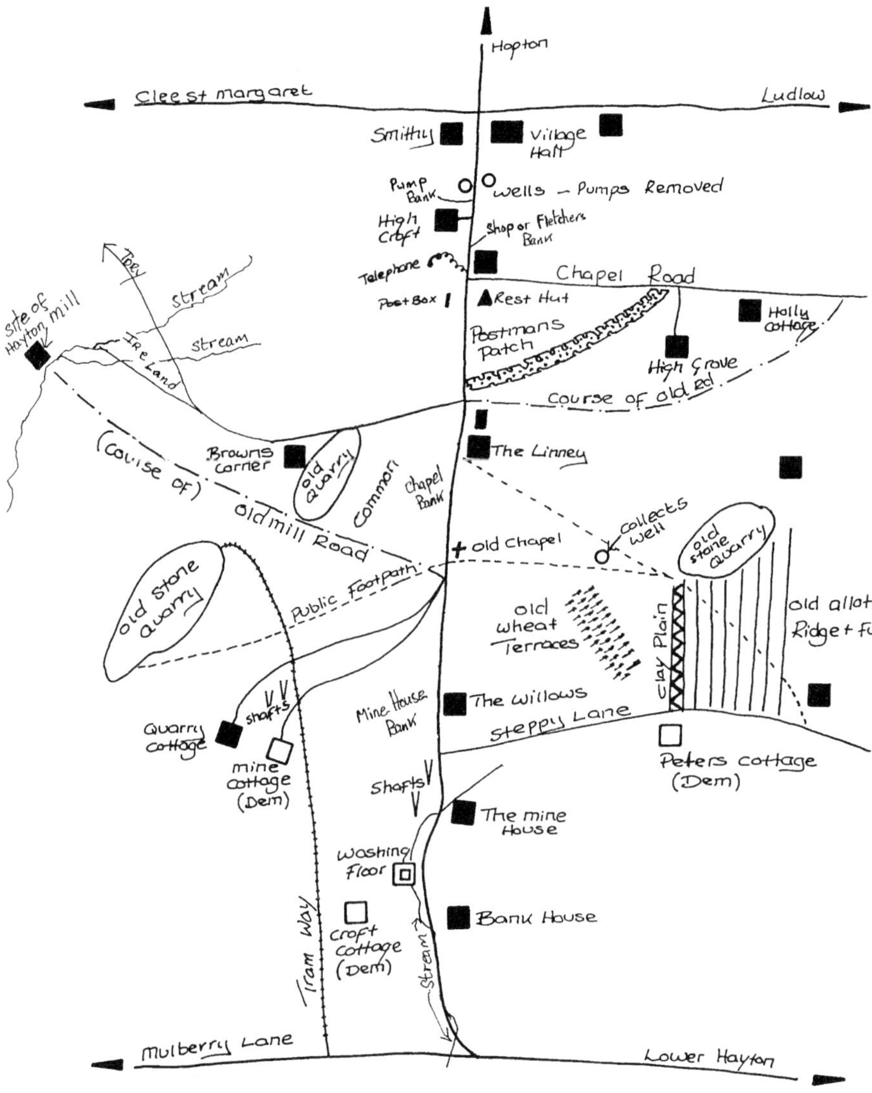

Map of Hayton Bank

CHAPTER IX

Hayton Bank

Hayton Bank runs from the junction of Mulberry Lane to the crossroads at the Village Hall. To make clear exactly where one is talking about, the road has been over the years split up into four parts: 'Mine House Bank' is that part from the bottom to the common gate, 'Chapel Bank' then runs from the common gate to 'Tory Lane', the next incline is known as 'Shop Bank' or 'Fletchers Bank', the last rise before the crossroads is 'Pump Bank'.

If you travel uphill from Upper Hayton in a south-easterly direction, the road passes through a deep cutting which is man made, the whole area being altered in the early 1800s, and again early in the present century after the steep sides of the cutting collapsed. During this last collapse a huge stone which weighed some five tons was deposited in the roadway; from whence this huge rock came remains a mystery.

The first house on Hayton Bank is the Bank House, a black and white cottage matching the Mansion House in age, and is thought to have been the lodge to that property. The road once ran along past the Bank House to the Mansion House before the cutting at the bottom of the Bank was driven through. The term Bank House had two meanings—either a dwelling built on, or into, a 'bank' as a hill in this part of the country is known, or in later years, a house built with monies borrowed from a bank and therefore the property of that bank until such times that the money was repaid in full. (This information may help to clear up the name of 'Bank House' when the dwelling is built on flat land without a 'bank' in sight!). Opposite the Bank House the old 'washing floor' from the copper mine can still be seen, just a raised platform surrounded with Harts Tongue ferns.

The Bank House, which was thatched until the 1930s. Chimneys on thatched cottages were swept from the top down to prevent the possibility of pushing burning soot onto the thatch. Hence the novel chimney with its steps, clearly the design of a particular mason. There were once four cottages with such chimneys, of which this is the last survivor. The chimney on the right is from a 1950s extension.

There once stood a cottage in the area around the washing floor where the copper ore was crushed and washed, but nothing of this dwelling remains. Turner's map of 1754 shows a cott here from which the field above would have taken its name—The Craft or Croft, both words meaning 'an enclosure with dwelling'. The survey of 1841 lists it as 'Upper Orchard and Garden', but makes no mention of a dwelling.

The Mine House

The next house, also on the right hand side, is the Mine House, which may have been connected with the copper mine at some time during its history, or may simply have taken its name from the presence of the mine. The 1960s survey of the Hayton Orefield, states that there is rumoured to be a 50ft shaft in the garden of the Mine House, but the shaft in question is situated in the garden of Mine Cottage, the remains of which can be found on the hillside above the orefield. (This is private property, but a public footpath crosses the area).

My mother's family owned and lived at the Mine House. Mother married from here in 1927, her marriage certificate showing that the Mine House was then known as the Miners Cottage.

The Mine House was once a butcher's shop, owned and run by the Bengry family, whose relatives still own the Mansion House. A slaughter house can be seen on the hillside above the Mine House garden. Mine House has been extended and improved in recent years, making it a very pleasant dwelling without spoiling its character.

On the opposite side of the road at the Mine House, tumps of Galena and Malachite could be found up until 1949 when Hayton Bank received its first complete metalling. Before 1949 the bank consisted of two runs of 3 inch

The Price family of the Mine House in the 1920s

Standing (left to right): Tom Price, Emily Price, Annie Stead Sitting: Mary Price and Elizabeth Price with children Stan, Reg and Millie Stead

Rick building

Dressed for Chapel: Annie Price, Mary Price, Emily Price (author's mother), Elizabeth Price and Thomas Price

riddled dhustone, one up each side, and one run of white limestone in the centre for the heavy horses to get a grip with their iron shod hooves. 'Dhu' comes from the Welsh for black; this stone was brought from the Clee Hill and Titterstone Quarries, whilst the limestone came from a local source.

On up Mine House bank, the lane on the right takes us up to 'The Bullring', along the top of Brand Hill and onto the Hope. Cattle were still being driven this way during the 1930s, and it was also used by pedlars and salters up to and during the Second World War. The lane got its name 'Steppy' not from the few stones that can now be seen, but from the regular earthen steps that are created by cattle when driven uphill. These earthen steps were once a feature, but have long been spoiled by surface water being turned down the lane, which has washed out the centre. The raised walkway can still be seen on the left hand side of the lane, but is grown over by the neglected hedge. The bottom of the lane where the overflow from Collects Well is piped underneath, again shows signs of collapsing. The area last collapsed in 1959, and was repaired by Shropshire County Council.

Returning to the Mine House bank, we continue uphill, where the next house on Mine House bank is The Willows, situated on the right hand side opposite the orefield, a well built pleasant building of some considerable age, with a 1950s addition. The survey and census of 1841 makes no mention of The Willows, but the building may well have been there; records do not appear to have been very accurate at that time. The owners of The Willows are descendants of old parish families, the female line can be traced in parish records back to around 1540.

The Common

At the end of the overgrown orefield we arrive at the common. This area was probably fenced in the 1850s when the William Lovett Mining Company made their survey for those gentlemen who hoped to mine copper here. Some local people claim that this area was once a large larch forest, gaining this idea from seeing the few odd European larch trees that have been planted on the old common, but this theory can be dismissed for two cast iron reasons:

(i) Rocque's map of 1772, Turner's map of 1754, Baugh's map of 1808 and all other survey maps from 1801 until 1848 show the area as being common land.

(ii) European Larch were introduced into Britain in 1620, but were only grown in 'Botanical Collections' up until 1790 when the first larch wood was planted in England.

The Powell family, who had purchased land from the Earl of Craven in 1862, planted the European larch and the Scots pine in boundary hedges to help mark out their lands. Evidence of this still exists in the areas around Sutton and Sutton Hill; those on Hayton Common were probably planted 130 years ago.

Quarry Cottage and Mine Cottage are situated on the lower side of the common below the quarry. Very little remains of Mine Cottage, but its neighbour Quarry Cottage has been modernized, and is now a comfortable home. There was once a tailor's shop attached to Quarry Cottage, a building now included in the conversion. On the female side, the owner occupiers of Quarry Cottage can trace their family back to around 1600 in Stanton Lacy and Diddlebury parishes.

☆ ☆

Returning to Hayton Bank, we see on our right hand side the Victorian Methodist Chapel (the old chapel on the accompanying map) built in 1847 and from which this part of the road has taken its local name, Chapel Bank. The building is disused, services having ceased here in the 1970s, and some of the roof cover has been removed leaving the building open to the elements, causing it to deteriorate rapidly. There are three wall plaques still in the chapel, commemorating those who gave financial help in its erection— John and Mary Bengry of Dale

A likely looking bunch—the Friswell brothers at the Common stile in the 1940s; (left to right): Doug, Trevor and Bill

View, the Halls and Harrington families, also of Hayton. At one end of the building there is a washhouse containing a fireplace and iron furnace, with a bucket toilet in another small building. Why a washhouse and a toilet when Chapel services usually lasted one hour? The reason lay with the so-called 'camp meetings' which were held twice a year outside each chapel and which could last all day. Water was boiled in the furnace to make tea; the necessity of a toilet is obvious!

At these open air meetings anyone who was committed to the Methodist movement and had a desire to speak could do so. These 'would be preachers' stood on high ground, if available, or in a cart specially brought in for the purpose. Many hilarious tales have been told down through time concerning these budding preachers. It is said that Tom, from the parish, a keen young 'Chapel goer' stood up to make his maiden speech at one of these camp meetings. 'Brethren, the World is round' said Tom, ''ers as round, ... as round, ... oh as round as a 'orse's yud.' Tom finished lamely, unable to think of anything that was round at that particular moment. On another occasion, Tom stood up in the back of a high sided cart to deliver a sermon. Being a diminutive figure of 4ft 10 inches, Tom could just be seen above the side of the cart. 'Brethren,' he cried, 'I am the Light of the World!' 'Turn the little bugger up a bit, he's burning in the socket!' came the reply from the outer circle, where Tom's cronies were standing.

In the field adjoining the chapel, Collects Well pours water from its overflow 52 weeks of the year, never running dry. Drinking water was carried from here to Mine Cottage and Quarry Cottage until the coming of the Severn Trent supply in 1962. Drinking water was also carried to all properties on the Bullring from the time their supply mysteriously dried up around 1840 until 1949, when a supply was laid on and pumped up by hydraulic ram from Collects Well. The water was pumped up to Yew Tree Cottage into a reservoir built specially for the job, then fed the houses lower down by gravity. This supply became redundant in 1962 when the Severn Trent supply was put through. (Although the Severn Trent supply made life in the country much more easy for the human population, it did, and in fact still is, having the opposite affect on the birds and small mammals. Thousands, or perhaps millions, countrywide, are drowned each year just trying to get a drink of water. Partly filled drinking tanks are death traps for our songbirds and small mammals. Before the piped supplies, many ditches, farm ponds and old watering stiles could be found throughout the countryside, but these were filled in, or were neglected and therefore silted up, making it impossible for birds to find water in hot weather except for drinking tanks. Larger birds and mammals will travel to water but not so small birds and mammals who live their entire lives in the area in which they were hatched or born.)

Returning to Chapel Bank, we climb up towards Hayton Bent, from the old Methodist Chapel to Tory Lane. Both grass verges during the summer are full of fire-flies, one of the few areas left locally where this once abundant insect can still be seen.

Situated at the top of Chapel Bank are three cottages on the right hand side. These were, until the 1960s, 1, 2 and 3 Hayton Bent. No.3 has more or less been rebuilt and named The Linney, 1 and 2 have been extended and modernized making all into comfortable homes.

Before the coming of the mains supply water was pumped by hand. This pump is wearing its winter coat to prevent it from freezing up

In the 1930s, there lived at No.1 a little old man by the name of Middleton, who appeared to hate everyone and everything besides himself. Being this way inclined, he, of course, had become a target for ridicule by the lads of the area. At Christmas 1939, the bigger lads decided that they would give him a couple of carols after he had gone to bed. He, like many old people living on their own in those days would be in bed by 8 o'clock. On this particular night some of us smaller boys were dragged along with the older lads to make a good strong choir and standing on the narrow yard by the only door to the property, we struck up. After a few lines, we were aware of the bedroom window above us being opened. The house was in complete darkness, there being only candles and paraffin lighting around at that time. As the window opened the older lads moved out towards the gate, still singing, but us small boys remained where we were. The contents of Old Middleton's chamber pot scored a direct hit from above. Soaked and shocked we raced out into the road with the old bugger's advice ringing in our ears—'divide that among ya!' By the stench of the contents thrown over us, it would appear that it had been saved for some time, perhaps he had saved it because he expected a visit. The carol singing may have been a yearly event, greeted with the same result—I never found out if this was so. This bitter old man died in 1940.

A much sadder event connected to No.1 Hayton Bent took place in 1944. Eric Cornes was called up into the army at the age of eighteen, and joined the Gloucestershire Regiment. Four months later he was killed at Caen shortly after the Normandy landings. Being a small community we all felt it badly.

From the top of Chapel Bank a lane on the left hand side leads down to a small farm known as Browns Corner. No one appears to have any idea how

A Spring Trap, common transport for going to church or market

this name came about. The simplest explanation would be that a family by the name of Brown once lived there, but there is nothing to support this theory. Between 1950 and 1979 Browns Corner was Hayton's post office, also selling tobacco, cigarettes and some confectionery. The female line of the present owners can claim to be related to very old Stanton Lacy parish families.

Retracing the way back from Browns Corner to the top of Chapel Bank, on the right hand side is evidence of stone quarrying in the field. At the top of Chapel Bank there are several yew trees. The lane from Browns Corner crossed over what is now the county council road running along the top of what is now the garden of No.1 Hayton Bent to join the Chapel Road near Holly Cottage.

Moving on up the road there is a Royal Mail collecting box situated on a post on our left hand side. Next can be seen a Shropshire County Council road sign with pointers telling us that it is Titterhill and Thriftwicket Lane leading to the Bullring. This is incorrect. Here on the left hand side of the road up until the early 1960s there existed the local watering stile where cattle were driven to drink in dry weather when other supplies had dried up. In earlier days when horses were the main transport they too were watered here.

To create a watering stile, the running supply was dammed at the lower end. A pool was dug out above the dam, which then filled with water. A stile with bars wide enough apart for cattle and horses to get their heads through was then erected across the mouth, thus enabling the animals to drink without treading up the bottom of the pool. Tree trunks were often placed along the mouth of the pools instead of stiles, the animals reaching over the top to drink.

This particular watering stile was fed by a spring situated in the yard of what is known as Pillar Box Farm. The overflow from the watering stile flowed on down the ditch to Browns Corner where it was again harnessed to supply that dwelling. It is noticeable that the supply is not reliable any more, the water from the ditch below the old watering stile has forced its way through the ditch bank and is running underground down the adjoining field.

Leaving the road junction and continuing on the road, the telephone kiosk is passed on the left hand side, with Pillar Box Farm opposite. This part of the road is Shop Bank, or Fletchers Bank, both names having been coined when High Croft was the local shop owned by the Fletcher family, there being one brother who farmed the small farm and three spinster sisters who looked after the shop. Most items could be bought here from the turn of the present century until 1944, when, due to the difficulty in obtaining supplies, the shop closed its door for the last time. This caused much hardship for the elderly and mothers with young families whose only alternative was to walk into Ludlow for their supplies, or wait until the once a week bus came through on Saturdays. Many families walked, because their small wage would not run to bus fares, especially if there were several children to pay for. Their menfolk, having to work half days on Saturdays (from 7 a.m. until 2 p.m.), then facing, in many cases, a long walk or bike ride home, arrived too tired or disinterested to look after a young family. The upbringing of the family was looked upon as womens' work in those days; the siring of children being looked upon as a man's only roll in family life.

Opposite High Croft, the hedgerows of the small fields are planted at regular intervals with oak, European larch, horse chestnut and hornbeams; oak and larch was used widely for building timber and estate work. The horse chestnut was probably planted for its fruits, but to what use these were put is unknown. But it is the presence of so many hornbeams (*Carpenus betulus*) that interests me. This was an important tree to the carpenter, its wood being used in the making of ox yokes, cogs, mallets, wooden screws and any other use where a tough wood, which did not split, was called for. Perhaps they were planted with the carpenter and wheelwright's shop at California in mind, (California was a smallholding with a carpenter's and wheelwright's shop; see the chapter on the Top road). The name 'hornbeam' survives from the Saxon period, 'horry' describing its tough heavy wood and its somewhat furrowed and fluted bark, 'beam' being the Saxon name for any tree species. There were until the mid-1930s two small larch plantations in this vicinity. One situated along the boundary with Pillar Box Farm fields, the other where these small fields meet up with land owned by Downton Hall Estates, which is clearly marked with a long row of hornbeams. Why these two small plantations were felled before the trees reached maturity is anyone's guess.

We now arrive at Pump Bank, the fourth and last rise of Hayton Bank. At the top of this short rise there existed until the 1960s two cast iron water pumps. A shaft had been sunk on the left hand side of the road at the turn of the century to supply water needed in the building of the 'New School', the supply then intended to provide drinking water for the school. But this source proved to be inadequate and unreliable and another well was sunk on the right hand side of the road. This proved a great success, the well never running dry during the hottest summers. Both iron pumps have disappeared, but the wells are just capped.

Jack Harris driving a bullock wagon advertising Atora Suet

Approaching the crossroads the new Village Hall and car park are on the right. Opposite these one can see a small horse chestnut tree (*Aesculus hippocastanum*). At this same spot there stood until the late 1930s a huge horse chestnut, and it was under the shade of this tree earlier in the century that the shoeing of bullocks took place, still remembered by my father and many of the older members of the community. The owner of the land found a 'bullock shoe' here in recent years when installing a post on which to hang the present iron gate.

From around 1910 until the mid-1920s the Atora Suet Company carried out a mammoth advertizing campaign, when covered wagons drawn by two or four bullocks (according to the area and terrain) toured the countryside to advertize Atora Suet. It is rumoured that several shoeing sites were set up around the parishes and that this site at Hayton was reopened for a brief period. Sam Curran of No.8 Stanton Lacy was the local bullock cart driver, touring the parishes of Bromfield, Stanton Lacy, Culmington, Diddlebury, Clee St. Margaret and Stoke St. Milborough in his brightly coloured wagon with its canvas covering advertizing Atora Suet in huge letters. Free samples of suet and tubs of beef dripping were handed out.

The Smithy and Toll House

The old Smithy is now used for an agricultural machinery repair workshop. The walls of this building are of some considerable age, though the roof is of a later period as it was once made of thatch, but was destroyed in a fire in the mid-1870s.

The house adjoining the Smithy was built in 1811 as a Tollhouse, when the Clee St. Margaret to Ludlow road became part of the Lower Ludlow toll system. The Ludlow Coat of Arms could once be seen on the wall of this building, but being worked in sandstone, it has now eroded away.

Edward Went was the last Blacksmith to operate the Smithy for the shoeing of horses. His wife was licenced to sell tobacco, cigarettes and confectionery from the house. Mrs. Went sold Fry's chocolate bars at ½d a bar, whilst Fletchers the shop and Mrs.Wadeley at the post office at High Grove sold Cadbury's, their cheapest bar being 1d. Us lads took our penny to the Smithy and got two bars of Fry's. This was seen by the sellers of Cadbury's as being unfair, the womenfolk from the post office and shop passing the poor unfortunate Mrs. Went with their noses in the air and not a word spoken! (Hayton's one and only price war?)

We have now reached the end of our journey up Hayton Bank.

CHAPTER X

Hayton Copper Mine

Hayton Copper Mine (OS 516810) is first mentioned by Murchison in his *Geology of Shropshire* published in 1839, (page 188), in which he states that the mine was abandoned around 1740 having never shown a profit.

There are indeed traces of old workings within the 'Psammosteus' limestones. Debris of grey calcareous sandstone and cornstone conglomerate can be found near two old shafts (SO 518811), 180 yards North 17^{0} West of the Methodist Chapel. The rocks bear malachite, and have been worked for copper in the past.

Hayton Copper Mine came into being about 1730, when samples of rock were taken from shallow experimental pits in the area. These samples were found to contain about 5% of copper, 13% being normally considered viable to mine. Nevertheless a horizontal shaft was driven into the hillside and a vertical shaft sunk further up the slope. However, as the workings proved very unstable and collapses were frequent, the project was abandoned!

Around 1850 Captain L.R. Carleston and Captain T.J. Penfold, Cornish mining engineers, were contracted by the William Lovett Mining Company to reopen the mine, to carry out a full survey and report in full on their findings. The surface landlord was the Earl of Craven, who backed the project in conjunction with the Earl of Powis, the Marquis of Bath and the Trustees of Lord Tankerville, all fresh from their success at the Westcott Copper Mine in the south-west Shropshire orefield. It was a time when many companies were set up and shares floated on the stock market; wealthy landowners often had irons in many fires! (Before the 1850s it had been necessary to apply through Parliament to obtain a licence to set up a company of shareholders. This procedure was an expensive and long drawn out affair.)

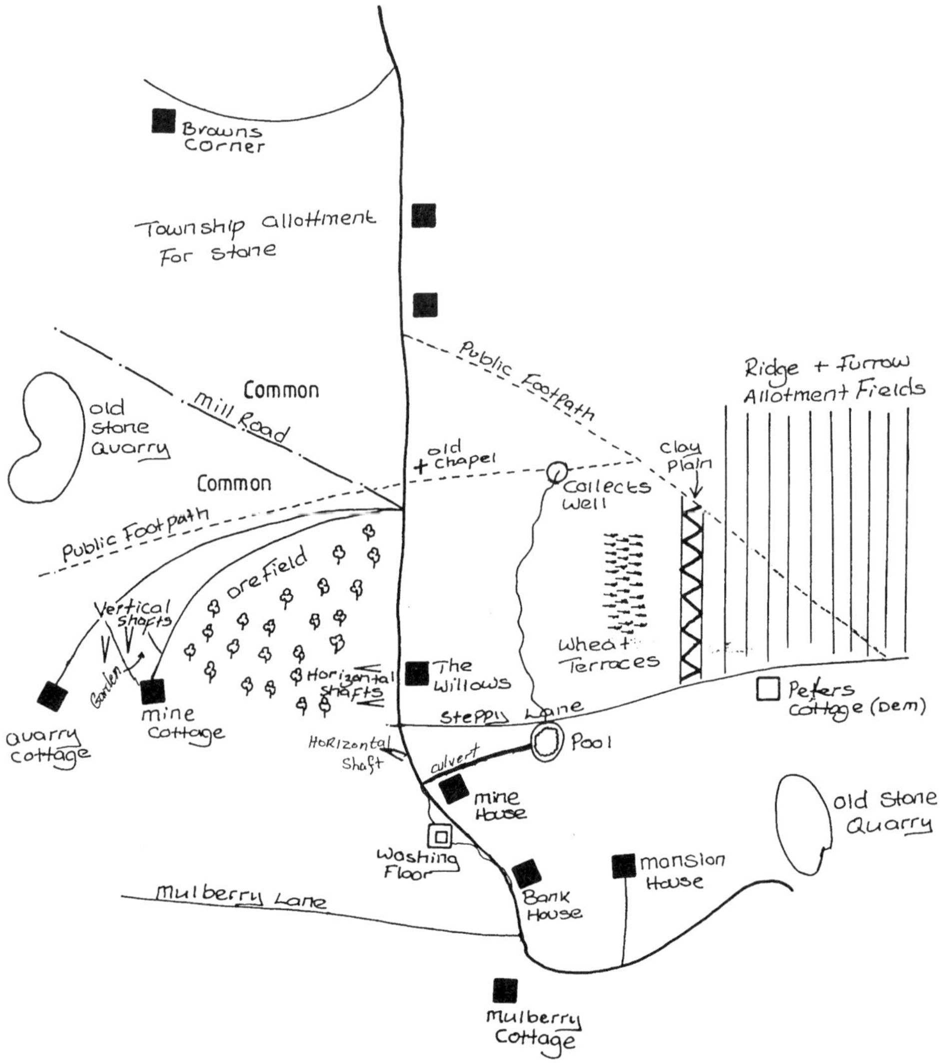

Map of Upper Hayton Copper Mine

The engineers opened up the Orefield at Hayton. They drove in another adit (horizontal shaft) from the roadside on Hayton Bank, and sunk a vertical shaft close to the one that already existed in the garden of Mine Cottage on the hillside above the orefield.

Collects Well, in the field by the Victorian chapel, was to play a leading role in this new attempt to find copper. The overflow from the well was piped under Steppy Lane, a catchment pool being dug on the lower side containing a sluice gate. A stone culvert was built to take the water down and under the road and into the field opposite the Mine House, where a small washing floor was set up to clean off the ore. Below this washing floor the stream passes back through the hedge and is forced to flow along the top of the man made bank by dry stone walling before flowing under the mouth of Mulberry Lane.

Captains Carleston and Penfold's report must have been unfavourable—the project was abandoned. The Earl of Craven sold the area including the orefield in 1862 to the Powell family of Sutton Court, though it is not clear if he also sold the mineral rights to the Powells or to the Earl of Powis. The Powell family made another attempt late in the 19th century to mine copper here, but the Earls of Powis still hold the mineral rights on most of the land in the area (1997). In the early 20th century the Powells made another attempt to mine copper, but met with little success, although ore was taken to an unknown destination in very small quantities. The records of the New Inn public house state that in 1901 its nature of trade was Mining, Agricultural and Roadside, 'mining' referring to the Hayton Orefield. What we cannot be certain of is, did the wagoners who were transporting the ore to Bromfield railway sidings, slacken their thirst at the New Inn, or did the miners lodge in some of its five bedrooms?

The *Birmingham Enterprise Club Transactions* for 1964 state:

> We spoke to the occupants of the cottages near the Methodist Chapel at Upper Hayton and were informed that in the 1870s the mine was worked by a labour force of up to 50 miners on shiftwork. A level was driven into the hillside to intersect old workings and veinstone containing both lead ore and malachite was extracted. The level was reopened in the first World War on a very small scale, finally closing in 1919.

If 50 miners had worked here on shiftwork, the area would have been covered with spoil heaps and some sign of their work would still remain. My family have lived in and around the area since 1365. My father, grandmother, great grandmother and great grandfather had recollections of the mining here from the 1850s until the final attempt during World War I. Their recollections were of two men with a wheelbarrow, each with pick and shovel; this being the working force of Hayton Copper Mine, the exceptions being that when a shaft was being driven in, a huge workforce was needed to cart away and clear the debris.

The orefield shows little sign of mining, because it never turned out to be a success during any of the four attempts to mine copper. Just two adits, two vertical shafts, one small washing floor, a handful of shallow pits where the ore outcropped at the surface and was followed down into the ground, a few barrow loads of waste, one stone on the washing floor with a single bore-hole proving that explosives were used here: these are the contents of Hayton Orefield. The extraction racks, which are in evidence at the top of the orefield, are in fact racks used to transport stone from the quarry on the Common opposite Quarry Cottage down to Hayton Bank and Mulberry Lane.

'Local Romantics' would have it that copper had been mined here for centuries, back to the time of the Romans. But this is not so! If one takes time to study Roman Britain in depth, there is no indication that they mined any metals in this part of the county. Evidence of the Romans having mined metals including copper can be found on the south-west Shropshire orefield, also at Clive Copper and Oswestry Copper Mines. Their method of mining was by drift; that is to say that they followed the vein from where it outcropped at the surface, going deeper as the deposits went lower. There is no evidence of any such drift mining having taken place at Hayton, only shallow surface pits.

To sum up, I will quote from the latest survey made by a mining engineer in 1995, brought in to assess the current viability of mining copper:

> At Upper Hayton trials were made for copper in the mid 18th century. Although a total failure, further explorations were carried out in the mid and late 19th century, and again during World War I. All explorations produced nothing worth recording.

The 1903 survey maps are the first to mention the copper mine, and refer to it as 'Old Copper Mine' suggesting that it was again abandoned at this time.

CHAPTER XI

Hayton School to Village Hall

Hayton School was built in1902-3, and was opened to pupils in the summer of 1903. The school was known locally as Hayton High, probably said with tongue in cheek as it referred to its lofty location rather than its academic successes. But the school had many boys and girls that passed their scholarship into Grammar School. Among these were my own brother and two sisters. Father said 'It's a poor family that won't produce one "Dull Bugger"!—And that looks like being our Cliff!'

The school was built on land given by the Downton Hall Estates. The site, according to Rocque's map of 1752, held a barn at that time, the adjoining field being 'barn piece', thus proving that this was not a part of the 'Bent' before the Enclosure Act of 1772.

Consisting of just one classroom and one small cloakroom, I would imagine that the school was always fairly crowded, the infant class being divided from the combined junior and senior class by two movable screens. Children moved up from the infants to the junior class at the age of eight, a teacher being responsible for both junior and senior classes at the same time. At the age of ten the child then moved to the senior class, to be set the same tasks as those in their last term at school, who were four years older. Seeing that all this was happening in one small room, it is not difficult for one to imagine the pressure put on the teachers.

In the 1930s the headmistress had a drink problem, some of the older lads being sent out to the local houses where beer was known to be made, to beg bottles of the stuff for Miss 'W' to consume in the classroom. This behaviour could not be allowed to continue. A meeting of the governors resulted in Miss 'W' being dismissed. This, of course, brought about more stress that

Hayton School , May 1937, in their production of the May Queen on the occasion of the Coronation of George VI. The lady with the fox fur is Lady D. Rouse-Boughton, school governor. The photograph includes all the classes

affected Miss 'W' so badly that she was admitted to a mental hospital. She was replaced by a Mrs. Williams.

The 1939-45 war brought about a great upheaval in many small backwaters like Hayton with the arrival of evacuees from Liverpool, London and Fleetwood. The school classes were swelled to bursting point, some 65 kids of all ages being squashed into this one small room. The majority of our kids came from Liverpool, were 'Liverpool Irish', and were Catholics. They brought with them their own Liverpool Irish teacher, a certain Miss Lilian S., who set up residence in the house next to the school, Mrs. Williams having been moved on previous to her arrival. It had been considered that these evacuees would feel more at home with a teacher from their own part of the globe; our old teacher, and us local kids did not appear to matter.The teacher moved on, and locals were thrown in with these strange kids who spoke a language of their own. In some cases the children's mothers arrived with their families, leaving their husbands back home to carry on with their jobs, or in some cases the husband was serving in the armed forces, or in one of 'His Majesty's Prisons'.

Few of the women stayed for any length of time, for they found the lonely countryside too much to bear, and returned to take their chances with the bombing rather than stay here. Some of them took their families back with them others took part of their family, leaving the older boys and girls to billet

Production of the May Queen, May 1937

with local people. Those partings must have been a great burden on both parents and children, but in our small world we did not give their feelings any thought, being only concerned with our own lives.

Many of these Liverpool kids were real terrors. Fights were many, we were more than outraged when a dispute between two lads often resulted with two or three setting about one. In our previous experience, if a dispute arose, then it was sorted out man to man, but not so these Liverpudlians. The whole family waded in, boys and girls. These kids swore at their teacher and at the local people whenever they felt like it. They stole cigarettes and sweets from the shop, smashed windows with stones and appeared to think that they could do just what pleased them and no more. Miss Fletcher at the shop soon noticed that things were being stolen and only allowed one child into the shop at any one time. We local kids did not care for being tarred with the same brush, but stuck to it, and the stealing came to an end. We took parties of the kids deep into the Cuckoo Pen, Stanton Lacy and Witchcot Woods, slipping away, leaving them completely lost. Many were the searches which had to be carried out to find them. This we felt helped to even things up. After a short period, things quietened down, and we were all pals together. Several of the lads stayed on after the war had ended, never going back to their native Liverpool except when visiting.

Miss S. was a different kettle of fish. She was hated by many of the local women, she chatted up their husbands, luring several into the school house.

All pupils, Hayton School, 1939
Back Row (left to right): Bob Tipton, David Evans, ?, Ruby Edwards, Dorothy Edwards, Mary LLoyd, Enid Baldwyn, Walter Smout
2nd Row: Bill Bailey, ?, Dorothy Tipton, ?, ?, Christine Baldwyn, Clifford Smout
3rd Row: ?, ?, John Lloyd, Maurice Williams, ?, Marjory Brown, Doreen Martin, Doreen Smout
4th Row: Margaret Lloyd, Bill Friswell, Bill Smith
Front Row: Isobel Cox, George Holland

'Ben', our local policeman, called there several times a week, leaving his bicycle propped against the wall for all to see. 'He'll be taking down a few small particulars!' said Dad.

There were no school dinners or school transport in those days, the school trawling its pupils from Hayton Bent, Upper Hayton, Hopton Gate, Red Furlongs, Downton Hall and the Hope, down as far as the chapel. The children below this point attended Stanton Lacy school. From the age of five we had to walk to school, carrying our dinners and, during the war, our gas mask. Smaller children were often bullied into carrying the lunch bags and gas masks of the bigger lads. Lunch usually consisted of bread and margarine, accompanied by a joint of rabbit, or a lump of fat bacon, which we were turned out of the classroom to eat at 12 o'clock, whatever the weather. On wet and snowy days we crowded into the small shelter for warmth, but it had been so erected that the rain and snow drove into it and the kids at the front got soaked. During the winter months we took a cocoa-sugar mix in a mustard tin with a small medicine bottle filled with milk for our 10 o'clock drink when a huge kettle of water was boiled on the open fire. The younger kids often got ambushed on their way to school, their tins of sweet sugar cocoa mix were plundered and their medicine bottles containing milk were often taken down a dose or two. This practice resulted in many fist fights between bigger brothers of the victims and the culprits. One day after I had been an early morning victim of such a raid and having nothing left on this occasion from which to make a drink, I took a bar of carbolic soap from the stand by the outside water tank, (this tank and soap were used for washing of hands), raced down to the school pump and rubbed the bar of carbolic round and round inside the spout of the pump. Two of the bigger girls took the huge kettle down to fill at the pump each day; this particular day was no exception and the resulting drinks were covered in bubbles with a very strong carbolic flavour. My delight was short lived: I had been seen replacing the soap on the stand. Two and two were added up, six strokes were the result, and I was mentioned in dispatches, by way of the punishment book.

The classroom had just one open fireplace situated on the west wall, with a wide chimney to take the coal smoke that was susceptible to blow back. We found this could be accelerated if the draught pipe, which entered from the outside into the chimney at the height of 4' 6" was obstructed. We used to push a folded cloth down the pipe when we considered that the wind was right. The thick yellow smoke from the coal blew back into the room getting thicker and thicker, until it was impossible to see. 'Outside children!' Miss S. would shout from somewhere in the vicinity of the fireplace, and we all struggled out into the playground. If the weather was fine, we would all go for a 'nature walk' down to the Cuckoo Pen or through Witchcot Wood, if the weather was wet or cold, we were sent home.

On these occasions, Miss S. would ask a couple of the lads who were in their last term at school to stay behind and help her with some chore in the school house. What these chores were I never found out at first hand, though second hand versions were plentiful, loud and colourful!

Bill, a lad who left school one summer term, delivered a dressed goose to Miss S. the following Christmas. The goose was to be taken back to her home in Liverpool for the family's Christmas dinner. Bill arrived with the goose one dark evening and, knocking at the door, he was invited to enter.

'There 'er was, sittin' in the owd zinc bath in front of the fire with 'er knees up to 'er gob. "Put it down on the table, and come and have a warm by the fire." Sez 'er.

I was rooted to the spot. "Pass us that there towel William!" Sez 'er raising up out of the waater so that I could get a good view of everything. Lors! 'Er looked jist like a skinned rabbit! I turns and bolts through the door, and makes for whoame!'

The behaviour of Miss S. was becoming the talking point of Hayton. The end came one particular day, when her temper had boiled over in the playground and ended with her slapping one of the big evacuee girls across the face. Several of the girls wrestled Miss S. to the ground. She was dragged into the shelter and secured to the central support post with skipping ropes; Mrs. Went from the Smithy came to see what all the commotion was about, the School Governors were informed and Miss S. was dismissed—much to the delight of the women folk!

The new head teacher was a Mrs. B., a miserable old battleaxe, who was chauffeur driven from Ludlow each day. We tried it on with her, but she was wise to most of our moves. I tried blocking up the draught pipe, but was canted on by a certain girl who wanted to get in with this new teacher. I was caned, and once more mentioned in dispatches. This 'cant' still lives at Hayton. If she ever reads this, I wonder if she will remember that day—now a half century or more past?

It would be wrong to think that all our time was spent larking about. We did our bit to help the war effort. Normal school lessons were waived in the early war years, and much of the time was spent collecting things—huge piles of scrap iron were formed in the playground of the school and down the Hope. Books for the soldiers and waste paper was collected from all the homes. The girls knitted gloves and scarves for the armed forces. During summer and early autumn we collected crab apples and blackberries which were then taken to the kitchens at Downton Hall to be made into jelly. The whole school would subsequently be marched to the Hall to act as a 'carrying party' to bring the jars of jelly back to the schoolroom, from where it was sold at 1/- (5p) per lb to our mothers and anyone else who wanted it, the proceeds going to the Red Cross. Sugar being strictly rationed, and the correct amount needed for the jelly to set being unavailable, the result was a jar of runny sticky liquid. Some of us would lag behind the main party and take a swig out of our jars, filling them up with clean 'ditch water' stirred in with a hazel stick from the hedge.

During these forays, we turned our attention to the ammunition boxes stored in the Nissen huts which decorated the roadsides, boxes containing cordite and other unprimed ammo. We carefully moved the boxes from one side of a hut, piling them neatly in the centre, and would then catch most of the rabbits that were between the boxes, or had scratched out short burrows in the dry soil underneath. The boxes were then placed back in their correct places, and the other side of the hut treated in the same way. The process would be repeated in a few weeks time, when more rabbits had taken over the territory of those already caught. A lookout was left in the road during these operations to keep his eye open for Frank Redworth, A.R.P. Warden, who came from Clee St. Margaret and patrolled a huge area on a pedal cycle.

The rabbits were sold in Ludlow for 2/6d (12½p) a couple. If we had had a good haul, we would play truant on a Friday and carry our rabbits, eggs (pheasants or pigeons), and other spoils, to Peaton, where we waited at the gates of the factories, selling our goods to the Brummies who were going home for the weekend. They would almost come to blows with one another over the purchasing of a couple of rabbits. 5/- (25p), they were prepared to pay, double the price of the Ludlow dealers. A cock pheasant would fetch 10/- (50p), a hen bird 7/6d (37½p), pigeons did not sell very well, a mere 1/- (5p) being top price. Eggs were 5/- (25p) per dozen. Seeing that many of these had been taken from under broody hens and in some cases must have been half incubated, we considered this to be a good price.

Peaton had two small factories during the war years, producing fuel tanks and other components for Hurricane and Spitfire aircraft. Experienced sheet metal workers were drafted in from the industrial Midlands. They were billeted with local families during the week, then were transported back by coach on Friday afternoons to spend the weekends with their families, returning to this area on Sunday afternoons, 'day light travel' being a must! These men were getting good money and had no objections to paying high prices for meat of any kind. They probably resold this back home, making a good profit, meat being strictly rationed, but this possibility did not bother us. Peaton factory closed in 1944, but the two security police boxes are still at the roadside.

The Rev. Robert R. Armitage, M.A., D.S.O., Vicar of Stanton Lacy took a keen interest in Hayton School. He had been an army chaplain, or padre, during the 1914-18 war, and arrived at 0900 hrs every Friday in his chauffeur driven, gleaming Austin 12. He called the register, and bullied the younger brothers or sisters of anyone who happened to be absent into telling him the real reason for their absence. (Many kids were made to stay at home to help with farmwork). He once tried the bullying technique on my youngest sister. Dad went to see him, and took him to task, after which our family was never bullied again. The Vicar ended these Friday morning visits by bellowing out

‘Onward Christian Soldiers’ until the roof shook. The old sweats said that his D.S.O. had been given for praying; the Royal Corps of Chaplains in which the Rev. Armitage had served was a ‘non combatant’ corps, so it could not have been for fighting! From a very young age, us lads were informed by the big lads that D.S.O. stood for ‘Dick shot off’, and that this had happened to the Vicar when he was serving in France. I well remember studying the old gent, and wondering in my young mind how the hell did the old bugger manage to pee without a dick?—So much for innocence!

Hayton School closed in 1946 and the kids were then bussed to Stanton Lacy School. Hayton School could probably claim to be one of the shortest lived schools in the county, with just a 43 year lifespan.

Calor gas lighting was installed in the redundant building and, for a small fee payable to Mr. Baker, agent for the Downton Hall Estates, the room could be hired for functions, the building which had been previously used as a Village Hall being due for demolition. The Mothers Union and the W.I. held their meetings here, whilst other activities included a Sunday School, Youth Club each Tuesday, dancing classes on Mondays, Army Cadet Force winter parades on Thursdays, and whist drives and dances on Fridays.

Dancing classes were hilarious affairs with Stan Byetheway from the Hope on the ‘squeezebox’ and Derek Hughes from the School House showing the steps. Many of us youths only had hobnailed boots to wear, or the lighter unshod tea drinkers, and we made one hell of a noise. Father once looked in just as I was trying to dance with a rather large girl who worked at Downton Hall. He informed me the next morning that in his opinion, I had looked like some bugger struggling to lift a ‘Gobsal-Brown sack’ filled with wheat. These sacks held 2½ cwt (130 kg) of wheat.

A kitchen was added to the old school after it was given by the Downton Hall Estates to the Parish as a Parish Hall in 1955. This building held many functions until it was replaced in 1995 by a new ‘Village Hall’. This hall is much larger than the original, with its own car park, but is not to everyone’s liking, being considered to be an ugly blot on the landscape in some circles. Time will mellow the building—and the minds of those that are dissatisfied!

The School House was built as a teacher’s house at the same time as the school in 1903. This is a tidy little house that looks younger than its years, the roof tiles and brickwork always looking fresh and new. Recent improvements have made it into a comfortable home.

CHAPTER XII

Hopton Gate
The Gate to the 'Hope Town'

The Settlement within the Narrow Valley!

Crossing over the Ludlow to Clee St. Margaret road you go downhill to Hopton Gate. A drive to the right leads down to Coppice Farm, passing Coppice Farm Cottage to the left. This was until recent years the workman's cottage for Coppice Farm.

There is evidence of stone quarrying at this point, building stone having been quarried here in large quantities. The waste was still being carted from here in the 1920s and 30s, and went into road foundations.

Hopton Gate consists of just four houses clustered together. It is evident that Ash Cottage was once a 'squatters cottage', it being plainly visible from the outer walls that both walls and therefore the roof have been raised. The house itself has now been renovated, with a red brick extension that does not really match the old dwelling! Exdale has been added to, making it into a much larger house than the small cottage that stood on this site. No.1 Hopton Gate is a charming 'old world cottage' that has lost none of its charm or features. The fourth and last house in Hopton Gate is the small farm, Hopton Gate Farm. The land once farmed from here is now attached to Coppice Farm.

Hopton Road was once gated here, giving the hamlet its name. One of the oak gateposts is still *in situ*. This gate was the official boundary between 'Bent Common' and the 'Demesne of Hopton', (Hopton from the 'Hope Town'—the settlement within the narrow valley. The small village of Hopton Cangeford in the parish of Stoke St. Milborough was once known as 'Hopton in the Hole', a vulgar name which no longer exists.

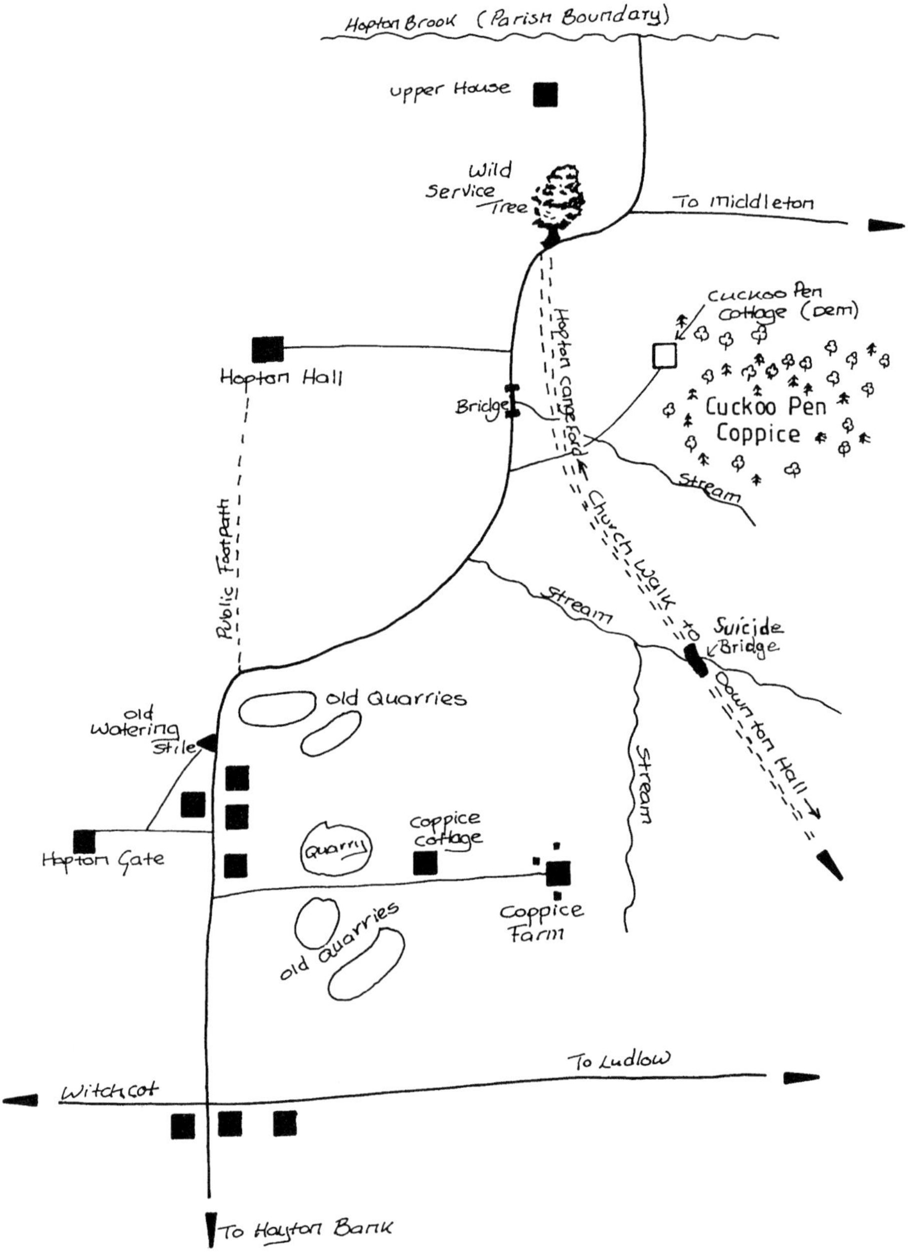

Map of Hopton Gate to Hopton Cangeford

Just below the garden of No.1 Hopton Gate, the local 'watering stile' can still be seen on the left hand side of the road, its pool now well and truly silted up. It is surprising how quickly these watering stiles have silted up, and in some cases have disappeared altogether in the 35 years since the Severn Trent piped supply was laid on. On the opposite side of the road there is evidence of more quarrying.

Journeying on down the road, 'Cuckoo Pen Coppice' is reached. On the right hand side of the road, up until the 1960s, the lovely old Cuckoo Pen Cottage stood in a clearing in the wood. Built as a Gamekeeper's cottage with its own small fields for the rearing of gamebird chicks, and to support a pony and house cow, this was a delightful spot to live, if one longed for peace and quiet. Sadly the cottage was demolished in the 1960s.

We must travel as far back as the time of the Druids to solve the mystery of the term 'Cuckoo Pen'. The Druids held most of their ceremonies in oak groves, as they worshiped that particular tree. Having no idea of seasons, they thought that trees died in autumn, and were born again each spring when the living spirit returned. The mistletoe, which at that time is said to have grown on oak trees, was highly worshiped because the Druids thought it held the secret of eternal life, being suspended between sky and earth and remaining green and bearing fruits when all around was dead. They were said to have cut mistletoe with golden sickles, clothed in white robes, a sign of purity, before laying the mistletoe around their altars prior to making sacrifices. White bulls were sacrificed to please the spirits, to make them return to the land that they had forsaken, or to make them return from the dead.

Then the cuckoo arrived in spring, bringing new life with him; the warm weather. New buds appeared on the dead trees, and the grass and flowers were born again with the arrival of this bird from the spirit world. The spirit died again in high summer, leaving behind a ripening, and therefore dying, harvest of corn, fruit, berries, fat beasts, and many other good things. If they could get this spirit of the cuckoo to stay throughout the year, then no more winter weather! No more would their fields and stores be empty, the trees would remain green, the flowers would be in constant bloom, and their world would be wonderful place in which to live. So sacrifices were held in oak groves to the spirit of the cuckoo to please it and persuade it to stay forever! This is the origin of the term Cuckoo Pen, there being many places with this name all over the British Isles.

The Church Walk from Downton Hall to Hopton Cangeford Church passed through 'Cuckoo Pen Coppice', the raised walk can still be seen in many places. An attractive footbridge took the walk over the deep ravine that runs through the wood, 'Suicide Bridge' was the local name. If it was considered to be a good place for one to commit suicide, or if such an act had once taken place here, is not clear—I can find no record of the latter!

On the opposite side of the road at the lower end of the Cuckoo Pen Coppice, a drive to the left leads to Hopton Hall. This was the main farm within the demesne of Hopton, an old well built building looking out over good well watered farmland, but open to the cold east winds blowing down from the Clees.

Hopton Cangeford, first a part of Stanton Lacy Parish, became a separate parish in around 1768 until it was recently merged with Stoke St. Milborough. The Cangeford part of the name comes from a Geoffrey de Cangefot who is mentioned in the records for the 13th century. Bishop Robert Burnell, Bishop of Bath and Wells, had also got his blood soaked hands on Hopton Cangeford by the year 1278.

The Green Family of Hopton Hall

The Greens on their arrival in 1903 at Hopton Hall from Clee St Margaret
Back Row (left to right): Margaret, Richard, Richard Junior, Thomas
Front Row: Edwin, Walter, Georgina

Left: The offspring in 1914, shortly before Walter, Edwin and Richard (who died in a German prisoner of war camp) enlisted in the army
Back Row (left to right): Walter, Edwin, Richard, Thomas
Front Row: An unnamed governess, Georgina

Right: Georgina in 1910. Note the single brake lever on the cycle

Below: The family in the 1920s

Richard Green with prize Hereford bull at Hopton Hall, 1910

Tom Green in the 1920s with a shirehorse, both dressed up for the show

CHAPTER XIII

Witchcot Road

From the Hayton Crossroads we head north-east along that part known for many years as Witchcot Road. Some 300 metres from the crossroads a drive on the right leads down to Clee View, a smallholding which, at the time of writing, is being renovated and extended. Clee View was once known locally as the Vicarage, so called after the Passey family who had lived here for many years, and had preached in local chapels, had formed and run a Sunday school, and were well and truly involved in the work of God. The last of the Passeys to live at Clee View, Aaron, together with his wife and nine children, struck out for a new life in 1903 when they emigrated to Australia. Nothing more was heard of the family until 1995, when two of Aaron's grandchildren, or maybe great grandchildren, arrived at Hayton looking for the old home. A time gap of 92 years, but it is nice to know that there was still interest in their roots in the old country!

The next dwelling on the right is a fairly new house, built on the site of an old cottage known as The Larches. Up until recent years this smallholding consisted of a few small fields: two of these fields were covered in the true wild daffodils in spring, but new farming methods and the use of artificial manures have killed this rare wild flower!

A lane to the left, Tory Lane, heads past Tory Cottage, a lovely old stone cottage, remaining unspoilt by its renovations. Further down the lane Tory Farm is reached, once known as Yew Tree Cottage, another smallholding. This area was known for many years as The Gold Coast, the smallholder of that time forever boasting about his 'ready money'. No evidence of this wealth was ever obvious!

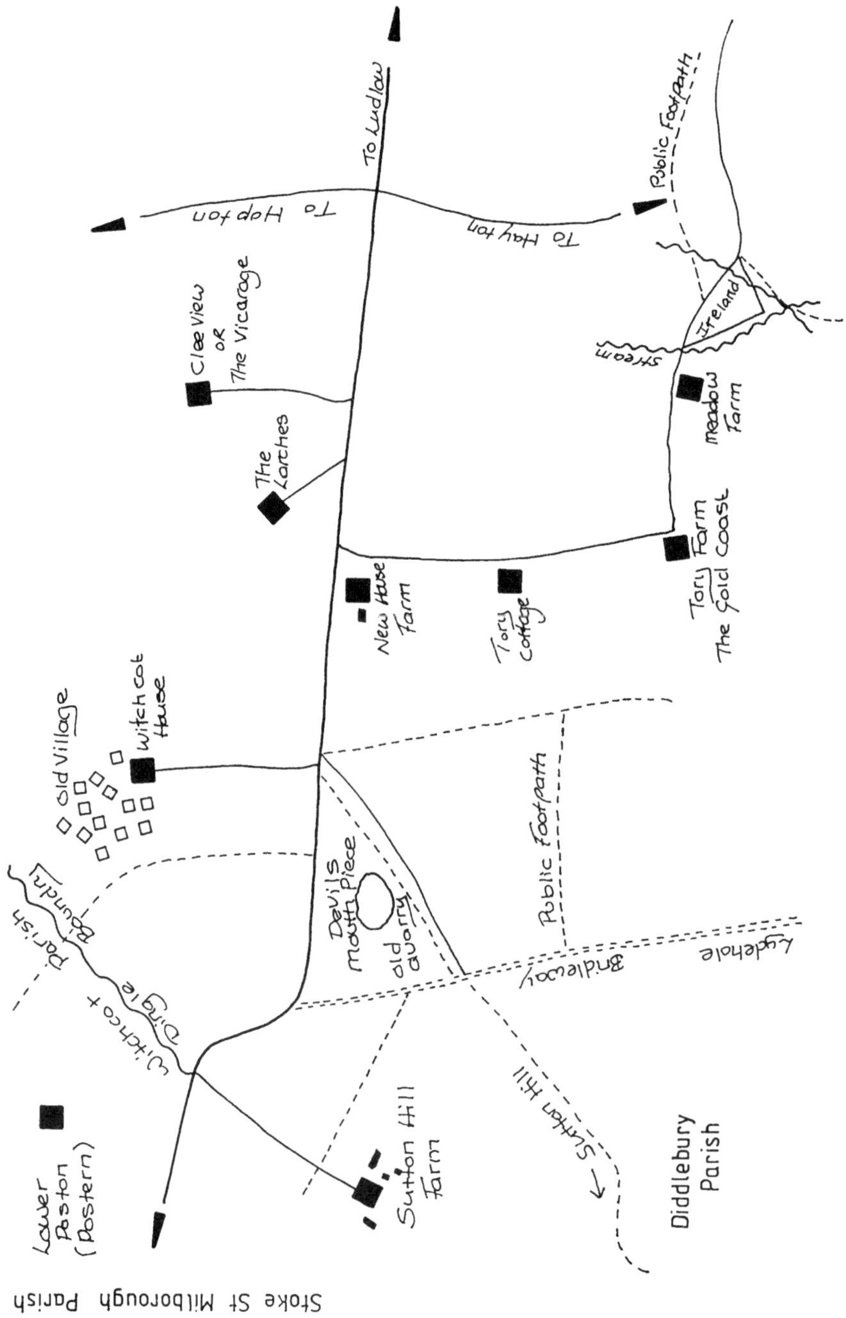

Map of the Witchcot Road

Journeying on, you arrive at another smallholding called Meadow Farm. The house has been modernized and extended into a comfortable home.

The metalled road ends here, but Tory Lane, an old drovers road, continues on to the top of Hayton Bank. The source of the Witchcot brook runs across the lane. This stream was once piped underneath the surface of the lane, but the brook is now destroying the public right of way. The name 'Tory' was originally the Irish name for a Roman Catholic outlaw, and in 1679 was applied to a supporter of the succession to the throne of the Roman Catholic James, Duke of York, later James II. 'Tory' has also become associated with placenames where the Irish had connections. Elsewhere in Shropshire there is a Tory Wood where the charcoal burners were said to have been Irish to a man; and Tory Coppice where it is claimed that Irish workers camped when working at a nearby quarry. It would seem safe to assume that Tory Lane therefore took its name from Irish drovers, especially as on its right and just beyond the brook is an overgrown patch of land called Ireland, probably the one time camping ground of Irish drovers. 'Tory' was no doubt a name given, slightly tongue in cheek, to these bands of drovers by local residents who presumably felt they were light fingered and who, it was claimed, would steal anything that was not nailed down.

Ireland is now home to one of our most threatened mammals, the dormouse. With the area now having become an E.S.A., (Environmentally Sensitive Area), it is hoped that this small area may be left as it is, to protect and encourage this beautiful little creature.

We must now retrace our steps to the Witchcot Road, having previously mentioned Browns Corner, the last dwelling on the lane. Back along the road, New House Farm is soon reached on the left. New House Farm, Witchcot Farm, The Larches and some other adjoining land are now run by a family who have farmed in the parish for many years. The New House has recently been extended, and these extensions have been blended in superbly with the existing building.

Further on is the drive down to Witchcot House, covered elsewhere in this book. Just behind the drive to Witchcot is 'Devils Mouth Piece', which until the 1940s was open to the road, and was the last remaining unfenced part of Sutton Common. It was then enclosed by the Church Commissioners, who had purchased the adjoining land from the P.G. Holder Estates, but it is doubtful if this enclosure was done legally.

Much has been written and surmised concerning the name of this patch of land, 'Will o the Wisp', 'Becky Smout Witch', 'Annie Potts Witch' and the

Devil all being linked with it. One poem suggests that 'Owd Nick', Becky Smout and Annie Potts danced and cavorted here together. One theory that the victims of the Black Death were buried here is absurd. The soil is fairly thin, covering solid rock: if any victims of the Black Death were buried in this area, the marshy ground at the top of Witchcot drive is the most likely place.

One will find fields and many other features of the county and country with the name 'devil' attached to them. When something turned out to be difficult to complete, old folk said the devil had made it so: 'devil's work'. For example:

Farmer to Workman: ''Ow be it working Garge?'

Workman: 'Not much Gaffer—it be as 'ard as the devil's foreyud!!! Or 'e 'ave bin 'ere right enough!'

Devil's ditch, devil's dyke, devil's den, devil's dream, devil's mouth, devil's nest, elve leasow, goblin piece, goblin yard, goblin stile, goblin meadow, Grimes piece, Grims meadow: these names are found in different parts of our county, all are associated with infertile or difficult land or terrain.

Right up until hand tools were more or less replaced by machinery in the 1950s, old men who used the scythe and sickle would hone their cutting tools to a fine edge before hanging them in the hedge ready to start the following morning. This practice was supposed to stop the devil riding the edge during the night. Some of the old men would mutter, 'If 'e do set 'is arse down on ha, 'e be in fer a nasty s'prize!' Reflecting now, these men must have thought he had called, finding no edge on their tools next morning, but this was due to mischievous lads spotting the tools and rubbing a copper penny down the edge, thus taking off all the cut. If the owner of the tools had left their 'cunts' behind, these were often filled with cow muck, but cunts were mostly left on the belts of the workmen. (A cunt is a sheepskin sheath for holding a sharpening stone, worn on a waist belt. The word is thought to be of Saxon origin). One may think that these were cruel tricks to play on older men—but the overall attitudes of these men were: 'Always kick a boy's arse, where ever you see him, because, if he isn't going to mischief, he's on his way back from it!'

As lads we often went to the 'Devil's Mouth Piece' at night when we considered the moon and wind were right for the job. There is a small disused stone quarry in the field, and when the wind gets trapped in this quarry it makes a ghostly whistling sound, which may be the origin of the 'devil's mouth'. We took with us some of the more timid members of our gang, which included evacuees, with the sole intention of scaring them, but in doing so we often scared ourselves. Approaching the quarry, we would listen for the sound of the trapped wind. Having picked up the sound, the bravest would creep to the edge of the quarry to see if we could see anything. A cry of 'Owd Nick!', 'Annie Potts!' or 'Becky Smout!' would send all off us over the rough ground, jumping the ditch which then formed the only boundary with the road, and off towards Hayton at great speed—all being shod with hobnailed boots, the sparks really did fly!

At the Sutton Hill end of the Devil's Mouth Piece, where the road turns sharply to the right, one can see a metal gate on the left hand side. Until the 1970s a lane ran from here down to Sutton Hill, with one branch to the Lydehole, when some 'ignorant immigrant', now departed from the area, had the double hedges bulldozed out and the public right of way destroyed. It is expected that a bridleway will be reinstated here in the near future. Just beyond the site of this old lane Stanton Lacy Parish ends. A new dwelling, Sutton Hill Farm, built in the field to our left is the last house in the parish.

Poston, on the right, was once in the Parish, but is now part of Stoke St. Milborough. 'Poston', once 'Postern'—the dwelling built on posts! Was this area once so wet that this practice was necessary?

Retracing one's steps back to the Village Hall, one cannot help but notice the wonderful views from the whole stretch of Witchcot Road. To the west can be seen much of the Corvedale with Wenlock Edge, the Longmynd with the Stiperstones peeping over the top, Warthill Burrow, Bury ditches, Blackhill, Hopton Titterhill and Blakeridge.

It could have been from this spot that the 'Great Man' himself wrote:

> Comrade, look you not into the West,
> Lest it tear the heart from your breast,
> Twill take your thoughts, and bury them far,
> Leagues, beyond the Sunset bar. (*A Shropshire Lad, A.E. Housman*)

But his visits to Shropshire are reputed to have been few and far between, so it is most unlikely that he ever trod this way!

To the east the Clees, to the south-east the Malverns, with Clows Top are visible.

A wonderful place to be is Hayton in spring, summer and autumn, but this whole area can change dramatically in winter.

CHAPTER XIV

Witchcott, Whychecott or Wychcott

Witchcott is now reduced to a single dwelling, its history having travelled a complete circle. Witchcott can be traced back to the mid-Saxon period, *c*.800A.D., and local belief that there once stood a witch's cottage here from whence Witchcott got its name, are completely unfounded! In simple truth the name means nothing more sinister than 'the dwelling in the elms', the Saxon term Wych was given to the 'supple tree' (*Ulnus glabra*), the wych elm. The tree was highly prized during the Saxon period as the slippery sap obtained from the young bark of the new twigs formed the basis of many of their potions. Indeed today the bark of the wych elm is used in pharmaceutical laxatives, know as 'slippery elm bark'. From the Saxon period when Witchcott appears to have been a single dwelling, until it was first mentioned in Domesday 1086, the history of Witchcott cannot be traced! Most historians claim that from the Conquest in 1066 until Witchcot became several holdings under free tenants in 1294, it had formed part of the Manor of Great Sutton, together with the deserted villages of Lesser and Greater Postern, now Poston and Cold Weston, hollow ways linking the old village of Witchcott to the 'Postons', Cold Weston, then Heath (a medieval village 3 miles from Cold Weston), Clee St. Margaret and Stoke St. Milborough. Other deserted villages within the area can still be traced proving that these villages were once thriving communities. By 1240 Witchcott had become a community large enough to support its own chapel and the village stood around the site where today's Witchcott House stands. This present dwelling is thought to date from around 1540.

In the mid-14th century, climatic change occurred, with both summers and winters becoming wetter and colder. Witchcott and other villages in the area were situated on an east facing slope at an altitude of around 230 metres (750 ft.). The change in climate led to loss of crops and murrain in sheep flocks, whilst the ravages of the Black Death all topped by heavy Royal taxation, made it virtually impossible to make a living. The overlords forced their tenants to clear and plant more land, so that the increasing demands for Royal taxation could be met. The tenants often had no option but to flee, leaving their lands and homes behind, and many such villages became deserted. From this time onwards much land was given over to pastoral farming, with extensive grazing land.

History tells us that Bishop Robert Burnell acquired the Manor of Witchcott in 1283 for a mere 100/- (£5). From this we gather that the land was worth very little, but perhaps we should note that it was a pillar of the Church who was purchasing, or forcing his unscrupulous will upon the people. Between 1294 and 1317, we find that a family had taken its name from the village of Witchcott. Geoffrey de Whychecott, and Hugh de Wych appear together with Thomas Brun (Brown) are listed as holding land in Witchcroft, Sutton and Over Hayton. In 1368 Wychcott lands were assessed at 2/- (10p). The Wychcott family were still holding the manor in 1450 when the land was taxed at 4/6d (22½p). In 1532 the land had been handed to Hamond Whychecott of Dunston, Lincolnshire, who leased the land that same year to Charles Foxe of the Inner Temple. Members of the Foxe family lived at Witchcott from 1532-1645. During this period Witchcott consisted of three dwellings: those of the Foxe family, John English and Sir Walter Long. The unpopular hearth tax of 1662 tells us that Witchcott had since been reduced to two dwellings, that of Sir Walter Long rated as nine hearths, and the dwelling of William English at three hearths, the Foxe family having moved to Bromfield parish, Charles Foxe becoming M.P. for Ludlow. The English family appear to have disappeared from history at this point, but they left behind lands that carried their name into the 19th century.

In 1665, Witchcott was let to William Herbert of Cilybebyl of Glamorgan for 99 years. Herbert was a partner in the Shropshire Iron Works, having married Mary, daughter of Richard Walker, 'Iron Master' of Wootton and Bringewood. William Herbert died in 1689 and Witchcott passed to another branch of the Herbert family, the Herberts of Oakley Park, Bromfield and Earls of Powis or Powys, and subsequently from them by marriage to the Cornwall family who held Witchcott from 1746-1846. By this time Witchcott had become a single dwelling with lands of around 410 acres.

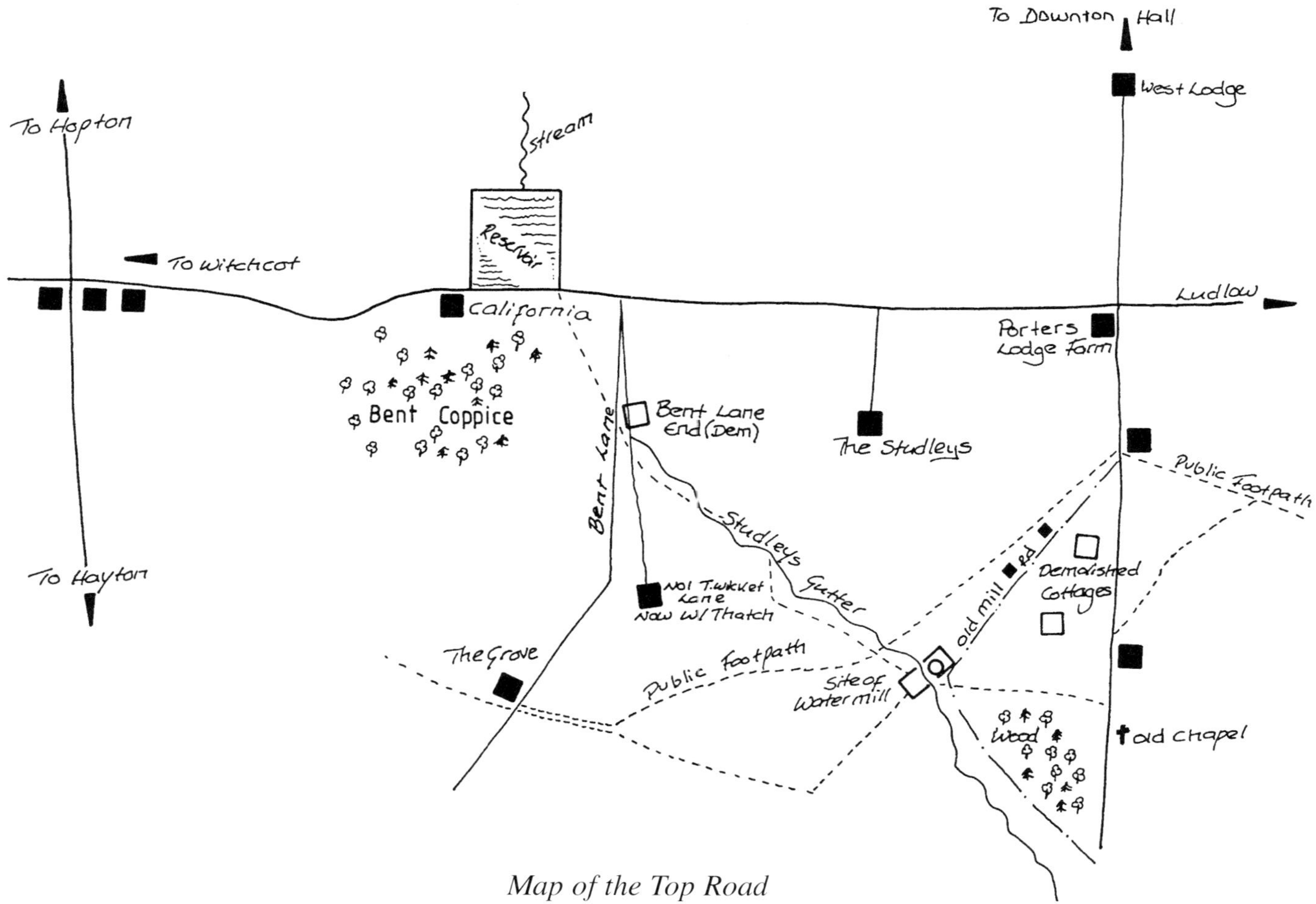

Map of the Top Road

CHAPTER XV

The Top Road

Striking out from the Village Hall we take that area of the Ludlow Road that has been known for generations as the 'Top Road'. This road is notorious for its ability to become blocked with snow in even an average winter. The winter of 1947 saw the snowdrifts so deep that they buried the telephone wires midway between the posts where the wires sagged at their lowest point, the result being that the weight of snow pulled the posts inwards snapping them off about 3 metres from ground level. After the thaw the G.P.O. laid the new line underground, the first stretch of county road in south Shropshire where this practice was carried out. During this time of great snowdrifts, if one moved 100 metres down the east facing slope, one found bare ground free from any snow; the harsh east winds, which have been known to bring tears to a 'glass eye' in this area, having piled up the snow, much like it does sand.

Heading along this part of the Top Road, one last reaches Hayton Bent, or Hayton Common. The Bent ran from Tory Lane, where it joined Sutton Common, to the Hope where it joined up with Short Wood Common. The small wood on the right is Bent Coppice, often called California, a name given to a small farm that joins the coppice. As Bent Coppice is mentioned at the time of Domesday and California was only built in 1849, I refer to it by its true and older name.

Bent Coppice supplied materials for hurdle making. It was also the place where the inhabitants of the township were allowed to collect firewood, a privilege enjoyed by many up to the early years of World War II, when Bent Coppice was initially clear felled. Under the old laws, which were harsh and unbending, the public were only allowed to gather dead wood that they could

The road cleared (above) after Martin Good of Holly Cottage, Hayton, cleared the snow (below) on 26 February 1955

pull down from the trees, hence the saying 'by hook or by crook'. The dead wood that had already fallen to the ground and was therefore easily collected, became the property of the overlord.

The coppice also became the place where the occupants of Hopton Gate, Thriftwicket Lane, and other dwellings, dumped their rubbish right up until Ludlow Rural District Council first started a refuse collection in this area in 1947. Evidence of these small dumps can still be seen. When the coppice was felled in 1941, all that was left was one beech and one sweet chestnut tree, both by the side of the public footpath, and both are still flourishing. If one examines the trunk of the beech the word 'PRICK' can be seen, carved into the bark. The carving has nearly grown over, but can still be seen if one looks closely. It was carved in 1938 when it stood out plainly for all to see and with Hayton Shop and Hayton School in full swing, many families travelled over the public path and considered it an outrage when they were faced with this obscenity. Small childrens' eyes were covered by a parent's hand as they scurried past. So much was made of this one word that John, the lad responsible, was expelled from Hayton School. A bad name travels fast and Stanton Lacy School refused to take John in. With no other school within sensible walking distance, John's parents, who owned and farmed the small-holding of Thriftwicket House, were more or less forced to sell up and moved to Whitchurch. John is no longer in the land of the living, but each time I pass this lone beech, with this one pathetic little word carved in its bark 59 years past, I think of it as his Epitaph. I wonder if these people, who pretended to be so outraged over this one little word, could return to see the graffiti that covers the walls of our towns and cities today would feel justified, knowing the hardships and distress that they caused one family so many years ago.

In the years after 1941, the whole of Bent Coppice became covered in raspberries, the canes seeming to spring from nowhere once the light got to the floor of the wood. The fruits were most welcome in those years of rationing and shortage—us kids picked baskets of fruits, carried them to Ludlow where they were sold, and returned home with bread and marge. We were all used to hard times brought about by the war. If there was a bus service that day, we would often decide if we should spend the 4d. which our parents had allowed us out of the proceeds on a bus ride home, or should we get ourselves a bag of chips and a bag of crisp batter? (No fish in those days). Being growing lads, with healthy appetites, we more often than not chose the grub, which was purchased from the Chip Shop at Quality Square. Our chips and batter were eaten before we were halfway down Corve Street; we then wished we had chosen the bus ride home!

At the time of writing Bent Coppice has recently been felled again, this time for firewood and fencing posts and stakes. Some species of trees have been left this time, the intention being to let the stumps shoot again, then they will be coppiced in 15 years. The bare open areas are to be planted with native broadleaves.

From its wall plaque, (if it still exists), on California we learn that it was built in 1849, the year of the Californian Gold Rush. News of the gold rush must have reached this far flung corner of Shropshire in time to so name this new house. The theory that California was built on the proceeds of gold mined in California cannot be correct if the information on the wall plaque is correct, for the Californian Gold Rush started in the summer of 1849, and it would have been an impossibility for anyone to have staked and registered a claim, mined gold, changed it into hard cash, taken a ship back to England, and built a house, all in four months! One may think that this is a trivial mater, but I wish to write relying on hard facts, not romantic supposition! In 1996 California was extended to make it into a larger and more comfortable home; the alterations have destroyed its character—but needs must!

The Rowe family lived at California for many years, operating a carpentry and wheelwright business, also undertaking and coffin making. The male line of this family has now died out and Stanton Lacy Parish is a poorer place with their passing.

Leaving California, on the left is a small rough patch of land. This is the head of Coppice Dingle, and a water supply enclosed in this rough area once supplied water for Coppice Farm, before the coming of the piped supply. Further on is a lane on the right, Bent Lane, but I will return here later.

Waiting for the Canting Cyart, Bent Lane end

Downton Hall Estates own the land on the left. A recent all weather gallop has been made to cater for the string of hurdlers and steeple-chasers that are trained here.

Further along, there is a drive on the right leading down to The Studleys, a new house built on the site of old Studley Cottage. Studley takes its name from the Old English '*Stubley*'—'the area

The parish slopes gently eastward with Titterstone Clee in the background

of woodland that has been felled to create a field'. Englishes Wood once covered much of this area, bordering both Short Wood Common and Bent Common on their western sides. Englishes Wood got its name from the family of that name who lived at Witchcot in the 17th century, and seem to have disappeared from history in the latter half of that century.

The Studleys had the distinction of being the only house in the parish to be damaged by enemy bombing during World War II. Thousands of German aircraft flew over this area on their way to bomb Liverpool, Manchester and Fleetwood, and Hayton was directly on their flight path. The bombers and their fighter escort followed the ribbon of the river Severn up into Worcestershire, then cut across country with the Clee hills to their right. We lay under the thatch at No.3 Thriftwicket listening to the drone of the bombers and the high pitched whine of the fighters as they passed directly overhead. We got used to this night after night when the weather and moon were right. One night, after a bombing group had passed over we relaxed, knowing that it would be sometime before we heard the empty aircraft returning, (the sound made by the bombers changed on their return journey, they did not drone so loudly when empty of their bombs), however, this one night in September 1940, the group had only passed over a minute before, when we heard the drone of a loaded bomber returning. The whining of its falling bombs and the crump-crumping noise as they exploded was one that we were unused to. The first bomb of the stick of 14 fell some 170 metres from our house. The explosion shook the building, breaking the crockery and mother's bits and pieces of china. The 14 bombs were dropped in a dead straight line from OS 518800 to OS 524787. Three of the bombs fell very close to Studley Cottage, blowing a huge hole in the rear wall of the building. Mrs. Tasker and her grandson Barry, evacuees from Fleetwood, were much distressed, and were found wandering by the Home Guard some hours later. A few days later the Tasker family rejoined the rest of their family in Fleetwood.

Why this bomber had returned to drop its bombs in this location is really an unexplained mystery. The searchlight battery at the top of the Hope had played its light on hundreds of enemy aircraft, trying in vain to dazzle the pilots. The searchlight battery had no anti-aircraft gun, so posed no real threat to anything. One theory was that the bomber had developed engine trouble and had turned back hoping to get to base. It would have dropped its bombs to lighten its load. It was rumoured at that time that the bomber had been shot down near Malvern after dropping its bombs at Hayton, but I have found no proof of this. Other bombs dropped at Lawton Farm and Tugford Village could have been attempts to destroy the small factories at Peaton—but the reason for the Hayton episode will always remain a mystery. The day following the bombing episode will always remain in my memory, I had never seen so many people before in my young life. Every field in which a bomb had dropped appeared to be filled with them; the whole population of Ludlow was there. They dug out shrapnel that had buried itself in the surrounding trees, taking this away as souvenirs. The Home Guard ran about like headless chickens trying to keep people out of the bomb craters. They warned of incendiary bombs lying buried, but no notice was taken of their warnings, which of course were false, craters formed by the explosions being plainly visible.

Returning to the top road we carry on towards the Hope. Approaching the top of the Hope we find on our right quite recent barn conversions. Comfortable homes have been made out of the old farmhouse and barns which once formed Porters Lodge Farm. This farm once belonged to the Downton Hall Estates, and the tenants had to fetch and carry to and from the Hall anything that needed horse drawn transport to do so. These present day conversions are out of place and certainly out of character with the area.

CHAPTER XVI

Downton Hall

Turning left at the top of the Hope, we find ourselves on the back drive to Downton Hall. The Heynes family were probably the builders of the present Downton Hall. They married into the Pearce family who in turn married into the Hall family when Elizabeth Hall, heiress of Stoke St. Milborough and Bitterley parishes, married Wredenhall Pearce of Downton Hall. They took the name of Pearce-Hall, their son William having one daughter, Catherine, who married Sir Charles William Boughton Rouse in 1782. They in turn took the name Rouse Boughton and the family held the estate for over 200 years, from 1782 to 1988. The Hall is built in Queen Anne style, and together with its surrounding buildings is, at the time of writing, undergoing major alterations.

On the right hand side of the drive approaching the West Lodge, the remains of the wartime searchlight battery earthworks can still be seen in the field. The battery was manned by a force of around 20 military personnel who lived in the Nissen huts on the site. A much larger Nissen hut formed the kitchens and Mess. It was this building that became the first Village Hall. When it was considered that there was no longer a danger of invasion, the personnel at the battery put on dances to encourage the population of the parish to relax. The military personnel left here in 1945, but the huts remained for several years after their departure, the Mess hut being used for whist drives and dances if permission was given. Seeing that Mr. Baker, land agent for the Estate, was the one who provided the music, I would imagine, that that was easily obtained. The huts, together with the Nissen huts that had been used for storing ammunition along the roadsides, were finally moved by the Royal Pioneer Corps in 1948-49.

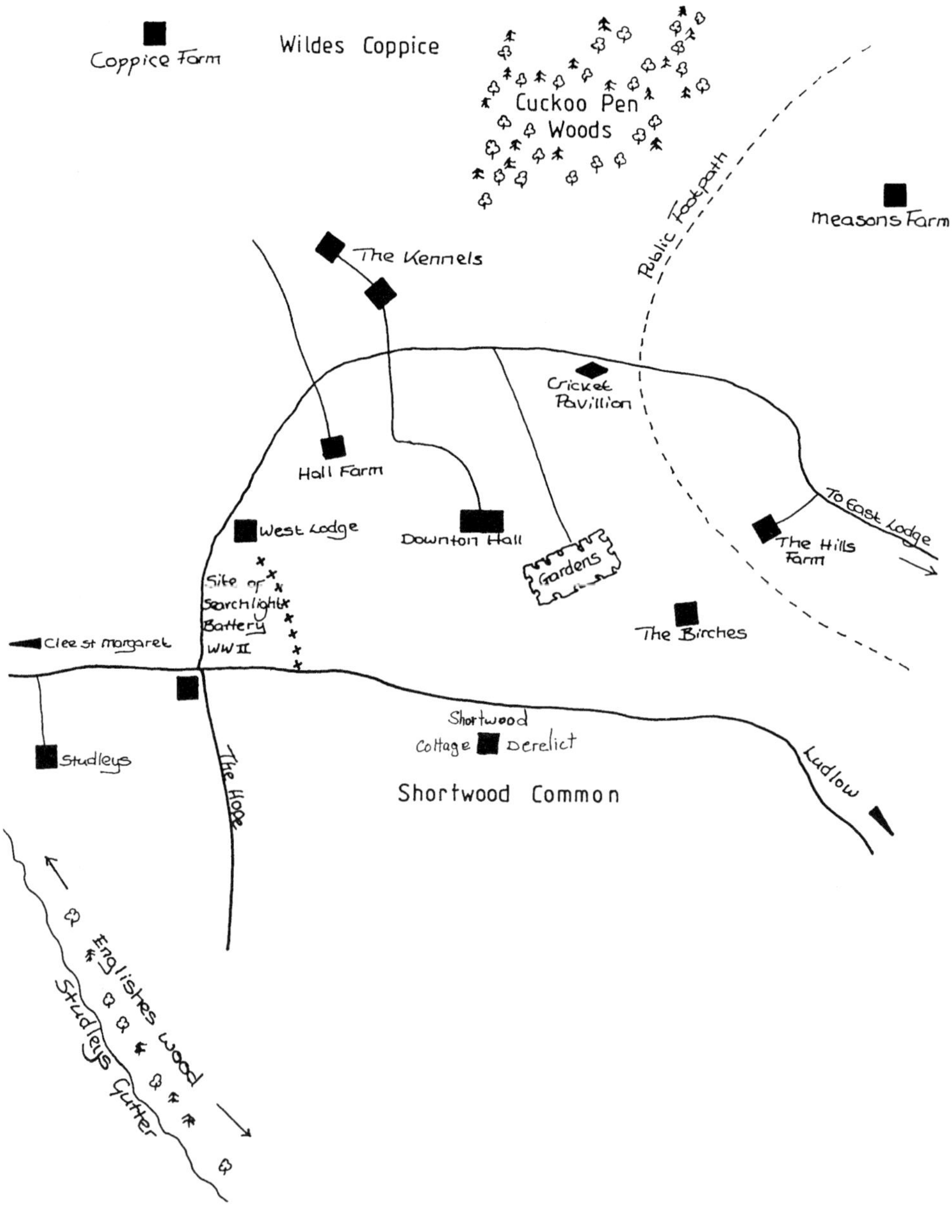

Map of Downton and Birches

The back drive to Downton Hall showing West Lodge which acted as the laundry for the Hall. The searchlight battery in World War II was situated in the field on the right

West Lodge was the Gatekeeper's House for the back drive. During the war it became the laundry for the skeleton staff at the Hall, and also for the occupants of the searchlight battery. The drive leads down to the Hall, which was once the main employer in the area: with its large stables, its own packs of fox hounds and beagles, its large gardens and kitchens, it employed some 30 people up to the outset of World War II. It once even boasted its own street—'Motor Street'.

The Churchway from Downton Hall to Hopton Cangeford Church. The bridge shown, Cuckoo Pen Bridge, was known locally as Suicide Bridge

Tenant farmers of the Downton Hall Estate with Sir Edward Rouse-Boughton outside the Hall in 1938 on the occasion of Miss Mary Rouse-Boughton's 21st birthday
Back Row (left to right): John Norgrove, Upper House; Percy Edwards, Lodge Farm; Edward James, Lower Wood; Fred Sanders, Upper Ledwyche; Cecil Corbett, Bank Farm; Fred Price, The Moor Farm; Edward Hayhurst, Littlewood Farm; Hedley Harris, Brook House Farm; John Evans, Measoms Farm; Bert Sanders, Quarry Farm; David John, Fishmoor Hall Land; Harry Brereton, Crow Leasows
Front Row: W. Williamson, Henley Hill Farm; Robert James, Coppice Farm; Stanley Evans, Lowbridge Farm; Richard Green, Hopton Hall; Sir Edward Rouse-Broughton; John Corbett, The Hills; Andrew Evans, The Measoms Farm; Thomas Randle, Old Vicarage; Edwin Jordan, The Paddocks

The Rouse Boughton family have now died out, ending what had been one of the main families of the parish for two hundred years. A relative of theirs now owns this estate, but I fear the old name has disappeared for ever!

The 'Birches', Downton Hall, is now marked by a single dwelling, but was once a small township under the Manor of Downton. By the year 1358, a

Life at Downton

Hay harvest near Downton Hall in 1918. Andrew Evans in the bowler hat with sons Jack and Stanley on the right

My mother's brother, Uncle Tom,with one of the Downton Hall pedigree Herefords in the 1920s

Downton Hall Beagle Pack, 1920. Sir Edward Rouse-Boughton holds the hand of his daughter, Mary, with Lady Rouse-Boughton on the right

family had taken its name from the township, when we find Sir Richard de Birches instituted on April 3rd 1358 to the Chapels of Hopton Cangenont (now Cangeford) and Ledewich. It is also rumoured that there once stood a mill at the Birches. Though I am unable to find or trace any records of this mill, one can be certain that the Birches and Downton could not have survived without a cornmill!

From the records of the 17th century, we can see that estate life is today still following the same pattern that it did some 300 years ago. There are those today as then, who would try to cause trouble for their neighbours by informing the estate's agents of any little thing that passed between their tenants. For Downton 1679:

> William Lloyd made an assault upon Evan servant of Richard Heynes and drew blood upon him, and the same Evan made an attack and assault on the same William. And that John Davies has sold bread and beer to travellers and therefore broken the assize. And that Joan Weaver (widow) has sold bread and beer and broken the assize.
> Punishments: Richard Lloyd find 1/6d. Evan find 1/- John Davies for selling bread and beer find 6d. Widow Weaver find 6d.

This 6d. was probably a larger sum than that obtained from the sale of bread and beer. There were estate trouble makers then as now.

The 63 members of Downton Hall Staff
January 1914

House
T. Marshall
M. Jones
S.M. Bathgate
E. Dickinson
H. Dixon
A. Rivers
S.A. Whitefoot
E. Hastings
A. Holms
F. Gough
J. Oakley
A. Morgan
W. Collings
L. Dudley
E. Lloyd
M. Evans
T. Stephens

Gamekeepers
P. Holloway (Head)
J. Floyd
W. Mound
W. Bailey
E. Taylor
P. Dickenson
J. Holloway
C. Holloway

Estate
T. Conway
A. Sanderson
H. Passey
B. Lloyd
H. Griffiths
H. Lane
C. Chamberlain
H. Hughes
W. Spruce
E. Norgrove ('Porter')
R. Overton
G. Edwards
R. Evans
W. Mound
T. Griffiths

Chauffeurs
H. Caisley
F. James
W. Thomas

Gardeners
L. Gill (Head Gardener)
A. Cowlett
M. Fishenden
T. Smout (My great uncle, Piddler Tom)
G. Perkins
J. Conley
A. Smout (My father)
H. Williams

Home Farm
J. Davies
Mrs. Davies (Dairy maid)
W.J. Davies
W.J. Grice
W. Passey
T. Perks
R. Davies
A. Howells
H. Ricketts
T. Williams
G. Hadley
E. Davies

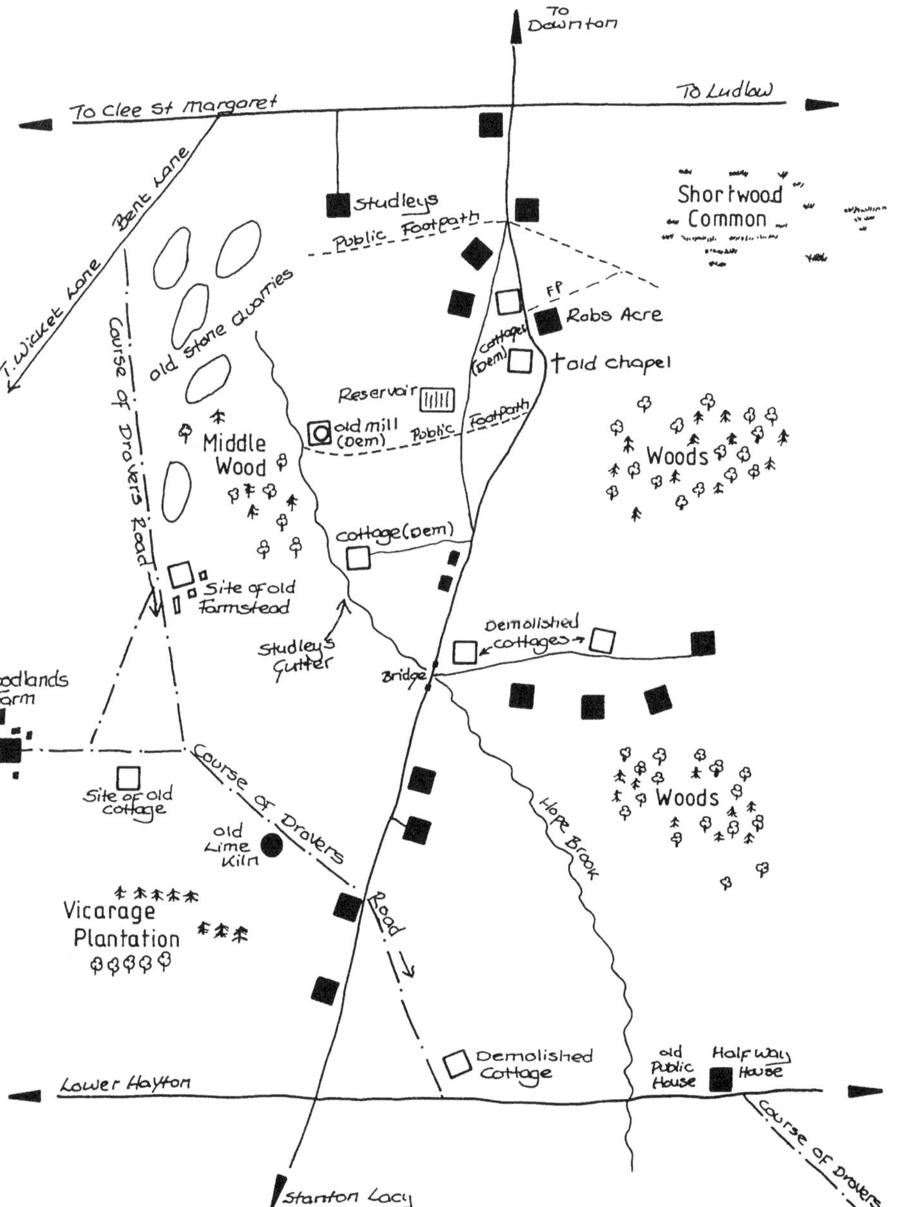

Map of The Hope

CHAPTER XVII

The Hope

Journeying down the Hope, the land on the left was once Short Wood Common, a name derived from the Old English meaning 'Flat-Wood', a term given to those areas of woodland that were regularly coppiced, therefore keeping the wood 'short' or 'flat'. From some of the field names that still exist we gather that many donkeys once grazed here—we find an 'Upper Dickey Stile', 'Lower Dickey Stile' and a 'Dickey House', Dickey being the old Shropshire name for Donkey! But why was a common used for the grazing of donkeys? We can only wonder!

The first houses reached were, until the 1960s, all workmen's houses for the Downton Hall Estates, four in number, one always being a double dwelling before being sold off by the Estate. Downton Hall Estate and the Plymouth Estates meet near here. An overgrown lane leads down the old Hope Road, rejoining the metalled road some 400 metres further on. The course of the Hope Road was altered after the closing of the Hope Mill early in the mid-18th century.

From the top end of this old lane, we carry on down the Hope road. On the right several small fields can be seen, once the orchards and gardens of the two thatched cottages that stood here until the early 1970s, themselves just two of the cottages that disappeared from the Hope at that time. There were eight in number, and were demolished to save the owners the expense of bringing them up to the living standard of those days. I am glad to add that this act of rash stupidity backfired with the property boom of the 1980s. These eight cottages with their gardens and orchards would have realised some £500,000. (So much for skill and forward planning!)

Hope Methodist Chapel, now in the process of becoming a private dwelling

Robs Acre, a lovely dwelling situated close to the Old Victorian Methodist Chapel was once a small thatched property belonging to the Estate; all those cottages demolished in the 1970s could now have been in this league if the money and imagination had been forthcoming.

Next to Robs Acre stands the chapel, now disused, and at the time of writing is privately owned and in the process of being turned into a dwelling. The chapel was built in 1862, closing in the 1980s due to a shortage of worshippers.

Moving into the wooded area of the Hope, on the left is a Norway spruce plantation, on the right a plantation of native broadleaves, mainly oak with a few ash interplanted. Further to our right beyond the Old Hope Road, now called Donkey Lane, Meadow Lane, or Mill Lane, we see a mature wood, Lime Kiln Wood, which forms part of Stanton Lacy Woods. The native broadleaves which form this crop consist mainly of oak, ash, sweet chestnut, and beech with a handful of European larch, hornbeam, Norway spruce and Corsican pine. The wood has reached maturity, and I fear it will suffer the same fate as the wood on the left, which was also mature broadleaves a few years back. However, with the forestry grants only being payable if a certain percentage of native broadleaves are included in the replanting programme, things may not turn out too badly. Two cottages on the right were once workmen's cottages. Three cottages stood here until the 1970s when the top cottage of the three was demolished. This too was a thatched dwelling, and the traditional yew tree still stands proudly near the old site.

Hope Brook, or Hope Gutter, now runs close to the road. This water course changes its name as it enters and exits the wood—above the wood it is known as Studleys Gutter, through the wood as Hope Gutter, below the wood as Hope Brook. A bridge built in the early 19th century takes us over the brook, there having been a ford here previous to the bridge. On the lower side of the bridge, the water cascades over a waterfall with quite a drop for such a small brook. The banks of the brook are covered in harts tongue ferns. A large patch of randsoms (wild garlic) flowers here in the spring; the stench of its leaves and flowers can be overpowering.

Stanton Lacy once was, and in some cases still is, supplied with water from Hope Gutter. A hydraulic ram situated near the old mill pumps the water into a reservoir, it is then fed down to Lower Hope and Stanton Lacy by gravity. This supply being somewhat unreliable in dry summers, I feel that much of the water supply needed is supplied by the Severn Trent.

A lane on our left at the top side of the bridge leads up to a group of houses with their small fields, large gardens and orchards. A further three thatched dwellings stood here until the 1970s. No.10 The Hope is a fine example of a long house, where the shelter for beasts joined the human living quarters, just a wall separating them. At the mouth of this lane, adjoining Hope bridge, there stood another dwelling with garden and orchard, but this site now forms part of a douglas fir plantation.

The road then leads into the Lower Hope and at this point the narrow valley broadens out into the Corvedale. Two cottages on the left have been extended and modernized. No.6 the Hope was one of those thatched cottages that escaped the bulldozer.

Below No.6 a lane on the right leads through Lime Kiln Wood to Woodlands Farm, which is the most isolated dwelling in the parish. One may wonder why this farm, with its house and buildings, was built here. The answer is simple, for the main Ludlow drovers' road passed through the yard of this farm. If we make Woodlands Farm our base, we can follow the line of the old drovers' roads for many miles. Turning towards Ludlow and travelling some 60 metres down Hope road the drovers' road then turned to the left, then down past No.3 the Hope (a black and white thatched property demolished in the 1970s), joining the present Ludlow Peaton road close to where the Hope Brook flows beneath the road, before turning left to the old Cider House, 'Halfway House'. (All 'Halfway Houses' throughout the country were once public houses). From this old pub the road ran away to the right where it joined the Ridgeway near Clay Felton. The Ridgeway then ran over the shoulder of Clee Hill to Bewdley, then on to Worcester and London, forming the main coaching road in that direction.

Heading in the opposite direction the Ridgeway led to Onibury, up green lane, over Brand Hill to Purslow, along the ridge of Blackhill over Clun and on into Wales, leaving Shropshire near Bettws-y-Crwyn, which translated

Harvest time at Woodlands Farm in the 1920s, Andrew Smout hands the cider horn to Tom Haycocks

into English is 'The Bede House of the Fleeces': the local bede (priest) would bless the sheep, or wool traders' fleeces on their journey over the Ridgeway.

Returning to Woodlands Farm and following the drovers' road in the opposite direction, it leads down to the Bullring which is said to have once been a market place, with a drovers' spring and watering stile and proof that a Cider House, now demolished, once existed. Across the Bullring the drovers' road reached the bottom of Hayton Bank, ran along Mulberry Lane to the ford, took the left hand fork down to Sutton and on to Sparchford, or followed the right hand fork from Sutton to Lawton, Diddlebury, and Middlehope, to join the Ridgeway at 'Round Oak'. From the ford at the end of Mulberry Lane, the right hand fork takes us up to Lydehole, along the Common to the old pub, The Hen and Ferret, now The Hen and Pheasant, and on to Peaton, where it was joined by the Burwarton Way. Left handed it ran to the old Cider House above Aston Munslow, the fording place on the River Corve can still be plainly seen, then on to join up with the Ridgeway.

The drovers' road was here long before Woodlands Farm. Turner's map of 1752 clearly shows the road, but there is no sign of a building. Many mounting blocks were positioned along the wall adjoining the dwelling, but were commandeered by the military to make tank traps during World War II. These mounting blocks, together with the huge cellar that once existed, may suggest that the Woodlands became a place to rest animals overnight along the drovers' road. Baugh's map of 1808 shows the site of a dwelling and buildings with pool at location OS 513795. Could this have been the old farm?

The area around the Woodlands was at one time a rough area, overgrown with bracken, brambles and gorse. These were cleared by the War-Ag in 1942 when the Pugh family took over the farm from Colin Philips. The farm is now a well managed holding. Proof that the Woodlands had been a rough overgrown area which had been cleared years before the 1942 session can be gathered from the names of several of its fields which form that area known as Brand Hill, a name given to areas of land cleared by 'the fire brand'.

Returning back down Lime Kiln bank, the remains of the Lime Kilns have all but disappeared. Near the bottom of the Hope lie No.5, a smallholding and No.4, which was once the gamekeeper's house. George Berry the gamekeeper, who lived here when I was a young lad, snared badgers. He salted down the hams of the sow badgers, much like those of the cottage pig. These he boiled at a later date and once gave Dad one to try. I could not bring myself to join in the feast, but the ham was eaten without my assistance. I would point out here that the snaring or taking of badgers in the late 1930s was not illegal!

At the very bottom of the Hope, on the left hand side, is a blackthorn patch. This was many years past the proposed site for a new Stanton Lacy Village Hall.

Lodge Farm and buildings. This was once called Porters Lodge Farm, and the tenants had to provide the horespower for transport to Downton Hall. It's now converted into several homes

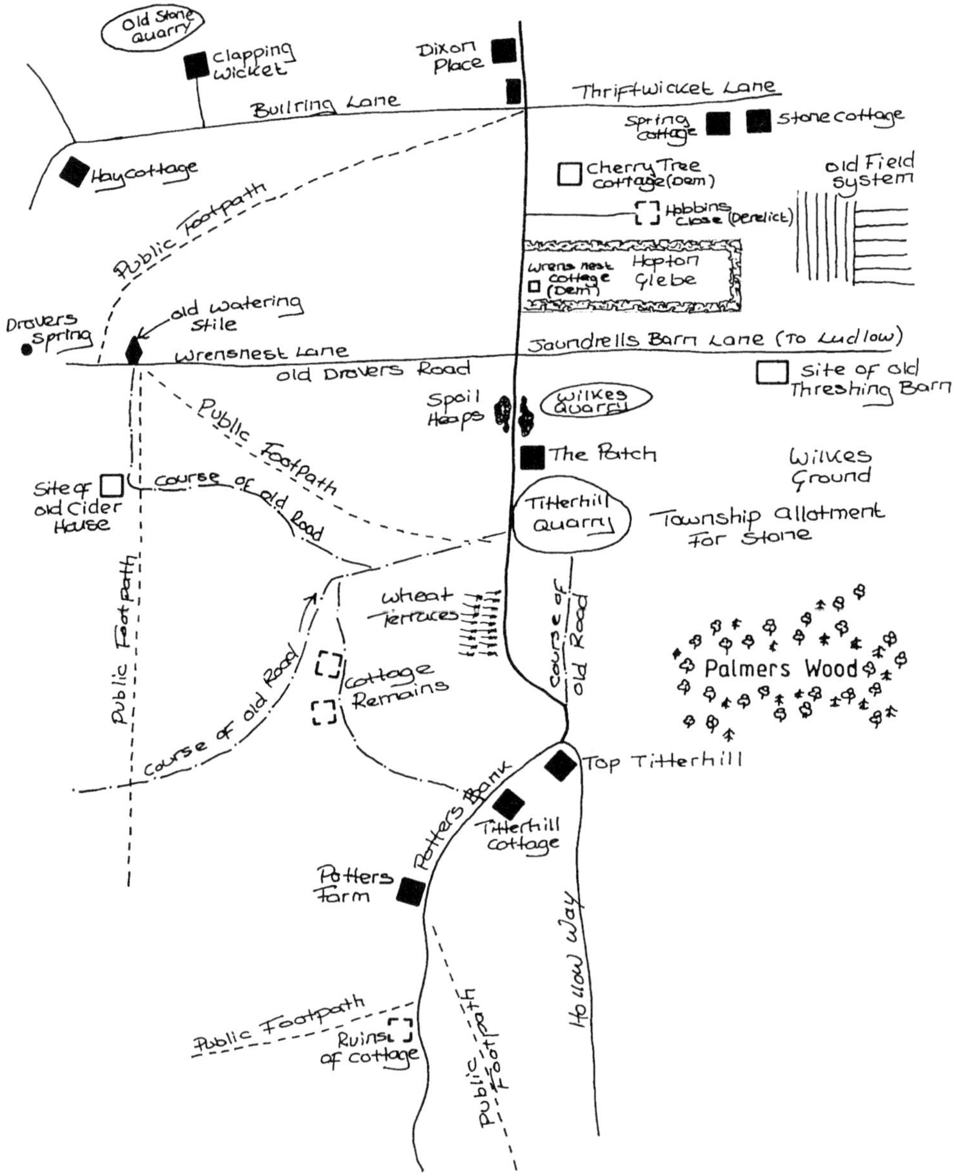

Map of Upper Titterhill

CHAPTER XVIII

Upper Titterhill

From the ruin of the old cottage situated on the left hand side of Titterhill Lane (from Teeter, to waver on the brink of falling), with its old baking oven still standing proudly and unsupported, the lane leads on up to Potters Farm, once a small farming unit, now a tree nursery supplying trees for both forestry and amenity needs.

The Bailey family have lived at Potters Farm for many years, a tough determined family who it has been my pleasure to know. If at any time during my life I had been asked to select a team to climb the highest mountain, or swim the deepest sea, my final selection would have included a Bailey from Potters Farm. Their dogged determination and persistence would have got them through anything.

Sadly, this grand old Hayton family were to suffer tragedies that they did not in any way deserve. Tom, the eldest son, was killed in 1944 while serving with the Warwickshire Yeomanry, and Robert, the father, also died in 1944 while still a comparatively young man. Jack, the second son, lost an eye but gained a Military Medal while he too was serving with the Warwickshire Yeomanry: a poor exchange, but one that was met and dealt with in the Bailey way! Philip, the third son, also lost an eye from an accident at work.

These tragic events would have been enough to have driven most families from Potters Farm, but not so this family. They just closed ranks, stood square on, rallied and prepared to face whatever adversity life could throw at them. Mrs. Ada Bailey stood at the head of the family, never shirking any duty, and as a staunch chapel-goer, she was prepared to meet anything with which her God saw fit to burden her.

Four members of this family of two daughters and four sons are still living, but none now live at Potters Farm, yet the Baileys of Potters Farm live on there, if not with the Bailey name. Janice, Robert Bailey's granddaughter, with her husband, John Holliday, daughter Lucy and son Tom, run the tree nursery. The house and surrounding area have been altered in recent years, the dwelling being extended and renovated, whilst the gardens and borders have been laid out to contain many of the rarer tree species.

Beyond Potters farm, Titterhill Lane is also known as Potters Bank, the steepest hill in the parish, so steep that the old county council steamrollers would not face it. Potters Bank only had its first real metalling and rolling a short time ago, when a diesel powered roller was able to manage this steep incline. During the 1920s and 1930s, this hill was used for hill climbing by a local car club. The area from below Potters Farm up to Titterhill Quarry was used on Sunday afternoons and evenings during the summer, with stop and start sections over its length, where points were awarded or deducted according to the quality of stops and hill starts made. Great fun was had by all, except the local residents who hated these events.

On Potters Bank lies Titterhill Cottage, an old dwelling which has not been altered by the addition of a bathroom and kitchen, still possessing its old world charm. Opposite the cottage stands a small barn. This building together with the fields now called The Banks belonged to Titterhill Cottage until the mid-1920s. My mother's family owned and farmed this holding during the early part of this century.

The next house on Titterhill is Top Titterhill, a recently renovated property which includes its own swimming pool. Opposite the cottage stands a plantation of Japanese larch, planted in 1938, the previous crop of oak and Scots pine having been felled in 1937. During this felling I, as a small boy, saw my first caterpillar which was being used to extract the timber. I spent many days watching this wonderful machine at work, wondering how the hell the driver could drive it without a steering wheel! The present crop of larch needs to be felled, not because it has reached maturity, but due to it suffering from butt-rot, and needs to be taken down while the timber still has some value. Underneath this overstory of larch, there are many plants of spurge laurel (*Daphne Laureola*), quite a rare species in this part of Britain.

Between the wood and the cottage, the old Hollow-way can be clearly seen. This takes us down to Lower Hayton, and was the only road here before Potters Bank was put through in the 19th century! Above the entrance to the wood the old road from Titterhill Quarry can be seen running close to the wood fence. This road suggests that stone was once taken from Titterhill, and maybe Wilkes Quarry, to Lower Hayton. This I have no doubt would have been stone for building.

In the field on the left at this point, one can still make out the 'wheat terraces' of the early 19th century.

Titterhill Quarry and Titterhill Lane

Titterhill Quarry was the quarry allotted to the townships of Hayton, both Upper and Lower, and Hayton Bent, where free stone could be taken by the local people for building purposes. This right still exists but sadly the stone supply is exhausted. There was also a community well of fresh water within the confines of the quarry from which local people obtained their drinking water. I am now unable to find the well, which appears to have been filled in though natural erosion and silting over the past 60 years. The quarry acted as a .22 rifle range for Hayton Platoon Army Cadet Force in the 1940s.

From the quarry, is a fine view of the upper reaches of the Corvedale, from its source at Bourton, down as far as Lower Hayton. It was such memories of views like this that prompted Ronald Colwill (1904-1986), then in self-exile, to write from the city:

CORVEDALE

The Sheltered Valley, folk there call the dale,
Quiet tapestry of meadow, plough and tree,
To the West climbs Wenlock Edge, to stem the gale,
Southward lies Ludlow with attendant Clees,
So Corve hill-fed by brooks that never fail,
Soon swells from muddy spring to swirling stream,
To wend a wandering way along the dale,
Sadly to drown in the more headlong Teme,
Thus a small river casts its magic spell,
Beyond the margins of a cradling land,
And quietly this loud century repels,
Rejecting the new trends as contraband,
Would there were more rivers in the State,
Our urban discontents to moderate.

The old Titterhill Lane ran down from the area known as Titterhill stile. Underneath the hedge where it forked some 70 metres from the present road, the left hand fork took one out towards Titterhill Cottage. Entering the road near the barn in the field already mentioned, the right hand fork ran along the top of the area known as Watkins Orchard, where there were two cottages to the Cider House. From there it joined Wrens Nest Lane opposite the watering stile. Another branch of the lane ran down the side of the present tree nursery, along the bottom of Balcony Bank and over Hopes Lane to join the Upper Hayton road between Sinks Corner and the White House. A small length of this lane's hedge is still visible at the end of Balcony Bank (OS 513811). All these old roads, lanes and rights of way are to be found on the principal triangulation map sheet 50, made by the surveyors Lt. Col. William Mudge and Captain Thomas Colby in 1811.

View over a snow covered Corvedale

Close by the quarry is a wooden bungalow called The Patch. This was never a 'Patchhouse', (a house that sold cider, bread and cheese whilst the womenfolk patched clothes whilst you waited, hence the name), but was built some 40 years past on the old quarry patch, an enclosed piece of land where the quarry workers for both Titterhill and Wilkes camped in their crude hovels made of wood, bracken and turves.

On up the lane, now known as Woodlands Road, we can see where the present Titterhill Lane was driven through the spoil heap from Wilkes Quarry, spewing some of the heap into the 'banks field' adjoining the tree nursery on the lower side of the road. This quarry is situated in the field above the lane and has also been worked out. After its closure, it was landscaped with sycamore, ash, elm and European larch. The sycamore, ash and just one European larch remain, the elms having all gone due to Dutch Elm disease. The European larch was a trademark of the Earls of Powis and the Powell family of Sutton Court, the former marking their boundaries with native broadleaves and European larch, while the Powells used European larch and Scots pine.

☆ ☆ ☆ ☆

A little further up the lane crosses over the old Ludlow road. The lane to the left is called Wrens Nest Lane and leads down to the Bullring, that to the right is known as Jaundrells Barn Lane after the Jaundrell family and the old threshing barn that stood in the field to the right of the lane.

With Evil Intent

It was at Jaundrells barn that I was to experience my first encounter with a frustrated woman, who had designs on my virginity.

Joan, a servant girl from Downton Hall walked the lanes around Hayton during her days and evenings off. She was a friendly girl aged about 18 years but had, however, been unfortunate when looks and figures were being handed out. Standing about 6 ft. tall, and weighing around 16 stones with a head like a 50 shilling pot, she was unattractive to the young bucks of the area, but one had to give Joan top marks for trying to get herself a man or boyfriend.

One summer evening in 1946, I was on my way home from Army Cadets. We had been on the .22 range at Titterhill Quarry and had noticed Joan hanging about. It had been my task to stay behind to clear away the targets after the parade had been dismissed and as I reached the mouth of Jaundrells Barn Lane, Joan stepped out into my path.

'Hello Clifford,' she purred, 'you do look smart in your uniform—you look like a real soldier!' My mind flashed back to what father, and his old 1914-18 comrades had said on their inspection of us some weeks before, but at this point I did not feel uneasy, not even when Joan asked me to walk up Jaundrells Barn Lane with her as we often used this way to the top of Thriftwicket. Approaching the barn, Joan took a firm grip on my right arm.

'Come into the barn,' she purred, 'I want to show you something.' Alarm bells began to ring, we were not as forward 50 years ago as young people are today, but I was aware how the act of sex was performed, and was eager to try it, but not with a girl with Joan's looks and figure.

'No!' I said, I've got to get going.'

Joan switched her grip on my arm to my neck. She had me in a head-lock that was both painful and suffocating. She thrust her face down to mine.

'Give me a kiss!' She demanded. Her lips were like two rolls of wet lino as she tried to kiss me. Failing in her attempt, she dragged me to the door of the barn and bundled me up on to the centre platform some 4 ft.. above the ground. I was gasping for air as Joan followed me in. It was surprising how agile she was for such a large girl. I noticed to my dismay that the door on the opposite side of the platform was tied up with binderstring; there being no escape that way, I turned to face Joan. She was sweating and blowing, and her face had changed—she now looked uglier than ever.

'Get your clothes off!' She ordered. 'You're going to do it if you want to or not!'

I took off my webbing belt, and started to undo the buttons of my battle-dress. Joan stepped out of her knickers. I well remember those knickers, they were blue in colour. In size they resembled two Gobsal-Brown wheat sacks stitched together.

'Hurry up!' Said Joan as I pretended to strip off my battle-blouse. Her eagerness was Joan's undoing. Rolling up her dress around her neck she settled down on her back on a few sacks that lay on the platform. She had no doubt paid an earlier visit to the barn, and had prepared her love nest, with the intention of snaring me, or one of the other lads, if possible. As Joan settled down, she looked like a large white sow, but now she was on her back I knew that I had won. Grabbing my webbing belt and her knickers, I crashed out through the unlatched door by which we had entered, to freedom. Once I was outside no one around could have caught me, least of all Joan. I could run like a park hare in those days!

I fled back down the lane like a scalded cat. Nearing the road a back-ward glance showed no pursuit. It was then that I realized I was still dragging those oversized knickers with me. Why I had taken them I had no idea, perhaps in the spur of the moment I had thought that Joan would not follow without her underwear. I wrapped a large stone into the one leg, tying the bottom in a knot, swinging them round and round my head, I let them go, they fled high and far, settling on top of a large thorn tree on the lower side of the road, where they remained until they rotted away. These knickers were the topic of conversation, many stories concerning their origin were put forward, but only two people knew the truth. I told no one, and I very much doubt that Joan ever did.

Joan and I never met again. She left Downton Hall soon after this incident. I hope that she found happiness and a man, wherever she went.

☆ ☆ ☆ ☆

The fields adjoining Jaundrells Barn Lane on the eastern side are known as Rickards Patches. At the top of the first field, ridge and furrow of the old field system are in evidence. This area together with the Wrens Nest Field, now part of Potters Farm Tree Nursery, were once known as Hopton Glebe. Maybe the church at Hopton drew some rents from this area. Hopton Cangeford became a separate parish with the building of its church in the later 1770s, but maybe someone who owned this land in those days gave this as glebe land to that Church—it is difficult to trace all these old records.

Wrens Nest Cottage and Clocky Bob

Very little evidence of Wrens Nest Cottage can now be seen. It was situated on the top side of Titterhill Lane, 20 metres from the entrance gate to the tree nursery. A very small one up, one down affair, hence the name Wrens Nest.

The last person to live here was a Londoner by the name of Robert Mason, a clock and watch repairer. Clocky, as he was known locally, fancied himself as a 'Member of Parliament' and it is recorded that after a few pints of Trouncers Ale at the New Inn, Clocky would rehearse his opening speech if an audience could be found. His speech included the following:

'My learned friends, my advice to you is this: "Never be backward in coming forward, or you will always be behind as you always were before."'

If Clocky's wildest dreams came true, and he ever became Chancellor of the Exchequer, his budget speech would include:

'Gentlemen, I propose to give to every man that works £1.00 per week, and to everyman that does not work £2.00 per week, the simple reason for my decision being that he who does not work will have far more time to spend his money in.'

Clocky's little thatched Wrens Nest Cottage burned down in the 1920s. It was claimed that a metal bucket filled with hot cinders had been left standing on a wooden floor under the stairs while Clocky made a two day visit to his native London. A day after his departure the house burned down. Clocky returned, collected the insurance money and departed the area, never to return!

☆ ☆ ☆ ☆

Travelling on up Titterhill Lane, an old cherry tree in the field on our right marks the garden of another cottage that stood here until the 1940s. This dwelling was one of timber frame with lath and plaster infilling. It was called Cherry Tree Cottage, which gives one an idea of the age of the tree—if the tree that still stands is in fact the original 'Cherry Tree', that is. I will add here that the Tithe and Apportionment maps of 1848-49 identify dwellings and holdings by numbers only. Names were only given much later when postal deliveries began in earnest.

All that remains to mark the site of Cherry Tree Cottage is the tree itself

To the right of this cherry tree, one can see the line of the lane that ran from Titterhill Lane to Hobbins Close. The hedge on the left hand side of this lane has been removed, but the lane can still be traced on the ground. A hanging post which once held the gate at the mouth of this lane is still *in situ*. Hobbins Close was a double dwelling, which has fallen into ruin, the families of Edwards and Wellings having deserted the property in 1915. The tile roof was stripped off in the 1950s, the walls were then taken down to their present level and a roof of corrugated iron was added, making the building into a shelter for livestock. Recent planning applications to turn the building back to a dwellinghouse have failed. The planning authorities state that it has always been a barn, but with two baking ovens, plus two inglenook fireplaces still in situ, one can only wonder at their judgement. Hobbins, Hobbley, Hobley, Hobbledy, Hobbly hurst (the wood with the Hobbes), The Hobbs, all derive from the Old English 'Hobbe', a name given to tussocks of bayonet grasses, which were once the bane of many meadows, having to be flayed off at ground level to rid the land of them.

Returning to Titterhill Lane, or Woodlands Road, as it is now known, we reach the cross lanes with Thriftwicket Lane to the right and Bullring Lane to the left. In front of us is the continuation of the county council road, Chapel Road, as it has been known since the Chapel was built some 170 years ago.

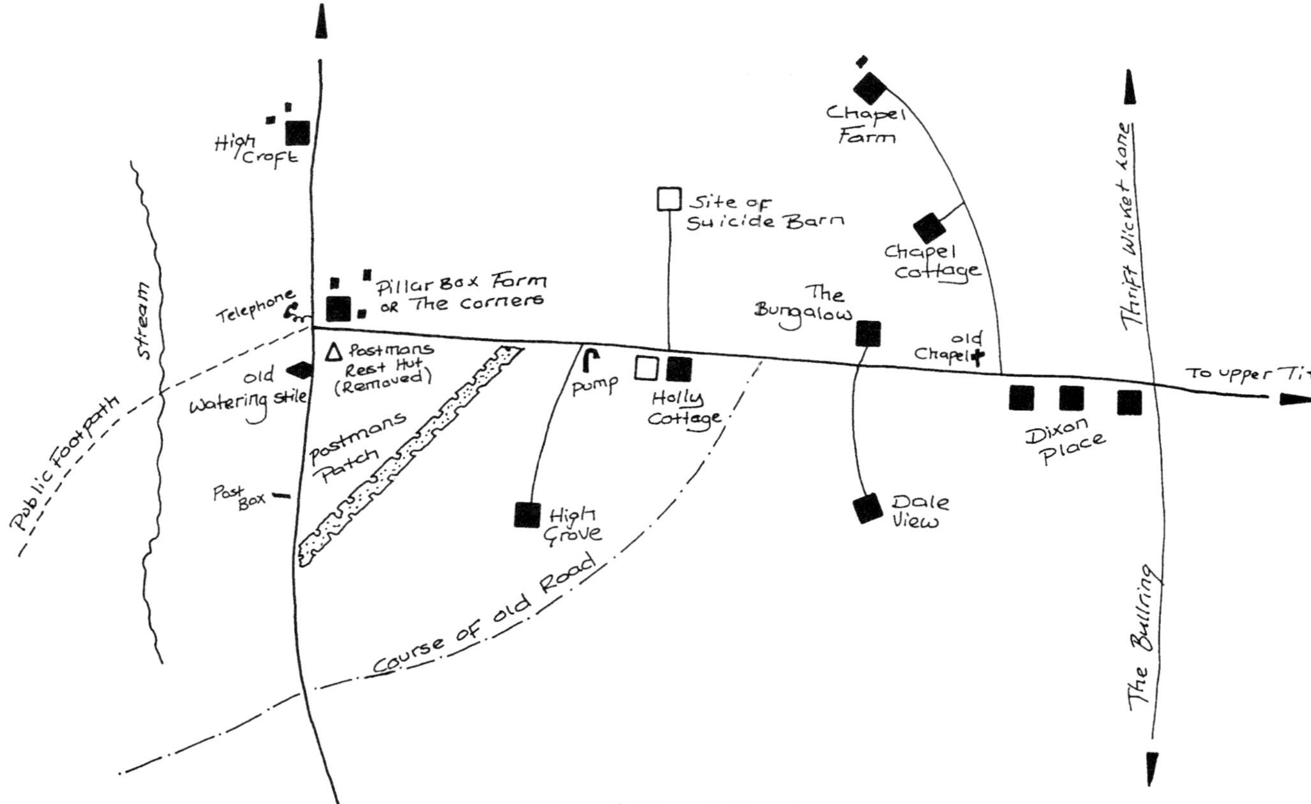

Map of Chapel Road

CHAPTER XIX

Chapel Road

The first house along Chapel Road is Dixon Place, built in the 1840s by, or for, the Rev. Lancelot Dixon. This was once a small farm, but now consists of the house, buildings, garden and one paddock. The house at the time of writing is undergoing renovations and extension. For many, many years, up until the 1950s, skimmed milk, butter, eggs, vinegar for pickling, paraffin and candles, could be purchased from Dixon Place.

The presence of the Reverend Lancelot Dixon in the parish yet with no mention of him in the church records, intrigued me and I set out to find out more. There was very little reference to the family: Lancelot had lived at Dixon Cottage in Thriftwicket Lane before, and during, the building of Dixon Place, moving to the new dwelling on its completion and in 1851 the Rev. Lancelot was mentioned in the census as farming at Dixon Place.

Still puzzled, I looked into the records of the surrounding parishes and here I was rewarded! The 1841 census of the tiny parish of Cold Weston lists its curate as one Reverend Lancelot Dixon. I feel sure this must be the same man; the name is unusual, there surely could not have been two in this sparsely populated area! I feel that the reverend must have commuted to his church whenever the need arose, for Cold Weston was then a parish of just some six or seven houses. He would, no doubt, have travelled on horseback, or horse and trap, or he may have walked, the journey of three miles each way being nothing in those days.

Just beyond Dixon Place lies the old Wesleyan Chapel. Built in the 1830s it was sold off in 1978 when lack of worshippers forced the Methodist movement to declare it redundant. It is now in use by Subud, a group who

Dixon Place being modernized

The Chapel-cum-School on Chapel Road. Now a building where Transcendental Meditation is practiced

practice transcendental meditation. The old chapel has had its past glories for, until the opening of the New Hayton School in 1903, this building was a chapel on Sundays, and a day school during the week.

Mary Bengry from Dale View was listed as the Day School Teacher in the 1881 census, but had been the teacher for a few years previously. My father started his schooling in the old chapel in 1899, but my great uncle Thomas Smout had started school here in the 1870s. The infants then sat in a half circle on the floor, scribbling on a piece of slate, or listening to a story from the Bible. Tom arrived at the day school on his first morning, and took his place on the floor with the others. During the morning Tom wanted to pee. Not knowing how to ask in this strange place and with strangers all around, Tom, no longer able to hold his water, stood up and peed down the back of the boy in front. He received a slap from the enraged teacher, Mrs. Bengry. After this, Tom waited his chance. When the only door in the building was opened for some reason or other, Tom made his dash for freedom, out of the door and off to the Bullring. That day saw the beginning and the end of Tom's schooling—he started aged five, and finished a few hours later. However, Tom's nickname lasted much longer than his schooling. He was known by some as 'Piddler Tom' right up to his death at Dale View Cottage in 1952.

The chapel was also home to a thriving Sunday School, a photograph of 1901 shows 50 children lined up outside the building one Sunday.

At the side of the Chapel, a drive leads up to a smallholding, Chapel Farm, a pleasant building with a more recent addition; outside there stands a fine weeping ash tree (*Fraximus Excelsior Pendula*). Chapel Farm was once known as the High House and was the home of the Edwards family. Lee Edwards was the Assistant Overseer or relieving officer, responsible for the Hayton Bent area. The overseer's job was to vet those who were living on parish relief. If in the overseer's opinion the 'paupers', as these poor unfortunate people were called, had become incapable of looking after themselves, they were taken into the Ludlow Union Workhouse. Families were torn apart by the decisions of these overseers, who do not appear as having any compassion, and very little sense. Couples who had been married for 50 years or more were taken, often by force

Chapel Farm, 1927, Martha Hodgeson and friend—both ladies had spent most of their lives as missionaries in India

into the workhouse. That was bad enough, but once in, they were parted for ever, the women in one wing, the men in another. After a half century in one another's company, these partings resulted in bringing about an early end to some; the attitudes of those in control were inhuman enough to hope that this would happen.

One old lady who had been 'taken in', as those forced into such a fate termed it, informed her daughter on one of the few visits allowed: ''Tis only for the rest of my life! If it was for any longer, I dunna think I should bear it!'

Chapel going looks to be serious business. Mary Price in Chapel black, 1918

Many sad stories are told of these old people's attempts to keep out of the 'Bastille', or the 'Grubber', as it was known. A man who was losing his sight would ask his wife to place things around the room where he knew exactly where they were. He would then exclaim when the overseer arrived: 'Well now—there's that penny I dropped yesterday!', picking the object up from the floor, thus hoping that his visitor would be convinced that his sight was perfectly alright. But I very much doubt that these fellows were easily fooled; they often came with the sole intention of getting the cottage back for the farmer or landlord now that the occupants were of no further use to them.

The Edwards family were said to have produced a string of these overseers, and are recorded as strutting about the area full of their own importance, swelled by the power they held over the less fortunate of the parish. The Edwards were said to have attended church or chapel as often as possible, proving what fine upstanding God-fearing members of the community they were. Perhaps when they passed on and reached their heaven, they may have been disappointed in what was proven to them.

The other night when I died,
The gates of heaven were opened wide
St. Peter in a gown of white, ushered me inside
And there to my astonishment,
Stood people I had labelled,
To be quite unfit, of little worth,
And spiritually disabled.
Indignant words sprang to my lips,
But never were set free,
Every face showed stunned surprise,
No one expected me! (*Anon.*)

What one thinks of oneself is unimportant, for unless a great majority of one's neighbours think you are as grand a fellow as you think you are, you are wasting your time when adopting a superior attitude. I would point out that I have mentioned the Edwards family because they were our local overseers; they were no different to the overseers of all other parishes.

On the left hand side of the drive that leads up to Chapel Farm, are the foundations of a dwelling now under construction. This building is being built on the side of a much older building, a one up, one down affair. These buildings, often termed one-up, one-down, were in fact two-up, two-down in that the downstairs consisted of one large room and a pantry, upstairs one bedroom with a smaller landing bedroom. The last family to live in this house before its rebuilding was one Tabler Hughes with his wife and seven children. The Hughes family moved from here around 1910, after which the property served as a cider-store house from that time under the ownership of Cider Billy Norgrove, until it was taken over by the Randell family in the 1940s when the old cottage was used simply as a store and tool shed.

Next to the old Chapel at the roadside stands The Bungalow. This was built around 1940 for Cider Billy, who had retired from farming and cider making in the late 1930s. Once a tiny affair, the building has had several extensions, and at the time of writing is undergoing yet more, which will make it into a larger and more comfortable home.

Dale View and The Evacuated Family from Liverpool

Dale View is situated down a short drive on the opposite side of the road to The Bungalow, and is a much improved and enlarged dwelling from that which stood here previously. John Bengry ran a shoemaking business from here and his wife, Mary, was a school teacher at the chapel.

During the 1939-45 war, the spinster who owned and lived at Dale View was forced by the laws that existed at that time, to give up one half of her home to evacuees. Indeed most country families were forced to take evacuee children into their homes, and look after them for a small allowance. But as Old Emma, the spinster, had only one arm, she was excused the duties of looking after children but had to turn over one half of her home instead.

Several families, mostly from Liverpool, came and went, some staying just a few days, or weeks, unable to stick the quietness of the country life! Then one strange family arrived and stayed for several months. They were Liverpool Irish and consisted of the mother, a woman of massive proportions, with her two sons and two daughters. From day one this family showed their intentions to be those of complete hostility to Old Emma and the rest of the inhabitants of Hayton. They bombarded everyone who passed along the road with a string of insults, delivered with an embellishment of filthy language that few in these parts had heard before.

The two sons were in their twenties and should have been serving King and Country. The daughters were younger, at a guess in their late teens, and they should have been working in the factories, or on the land. No one in those days was allowed to be without a job, but somehow this family had escaped the net. One would have thought that had they been hiding from their expected duties, they would not have drawn attention to themselves in the way they did.

Many complaints were made concerning the behaviour of this unpleasant family. Ben, our local policeman, was sent in to order them to mend their ways, but met with the same hostile reception as everyone else, and abandoned the task.

Dad said: 'I've had enough of it. I didna fight in the last un to create a country for bastards like them to live in and act as they be. I'll sort the bloody lot out!'

'And I'm with ya!' Said Alfred his lifelong friend. 'We'll stop 'em once and for all!'

A plot was hatched. Alfred and I were to hide in the hedge a short distance from the front gate to Dale View, while Dad was to go on along the road, as they only attacked lone men and women or groups of children. Dad walked on, and sure enough the family piled out of the house; one of them always appeared to be on watch for victims passing by. A mouthful of threats and abuse greeted dad. He had been a 'cruiserweight' Army boxing champion and had a left hook that it was said could stop a Hereford bull in its tracks.

The family were taken aback when Dad said 'Come on then you bastards! I'll take the bloody lot of you!' They had been used to people hurrying on, ignoring them, making them feel that they had won the day. The two girls retreated into the garden. Dad set about the two young men, who did not last many seconds, but the old woman was made of stronger stuff, being armed with a four foot length of broomstick. She cracked Alfred, who had now joined Dad at the scene, across the face, laying his cheek below the eye open to the bone. With a mouthful of triumphant filth she turned her attention to dad, but he was far too quick for her, stepping inside her flailing arms, he half lifted her, half threw her on to her back into the deep ditch at the roadside, from whence she gathered herself up, and finding that she had been disarmed, retreated to the safety of the house to join the rest of her brood who had already sought safety there.

'Christ Alfred!' Said Dad when things had been sorted out, 'I think the owd bugger is a mon dressed up to look like a 'ooman the way 'er fought!]

'Na' said Alfred, 'you be wrong there Andrew, 'ers a 'ooman alright! I did ketch a glimpse of the holyland as 'er box-snecked arse over yud into the ditch. 'Er 'ad got no draws on. Oh ah! 'Ers a 'ooman alright!'

That incident was the end of the family as far as Hayton was concerned. A week later they had disappeared from the area.

Father was held up as a hero by Old Emma, and the rest of the female population of Hayton for having rid them of these objectionable people. Many of the menfolk muttered that they would have made a better job of things had it been left to them, others muttered that they did not hold with a man rough handling a woman. The opportunity had existed for them to have done something about their plight in the months leading up to the final incident, but as Dad said on hearing of these mutterings, 'Talk is cheap, any bugger can talk a good fight!'

☆ ☆ ☆ ☆

Moving on along the road we reach Holly Cottage, a charming stone building unspoiled by excessive renovations and extensions, just a bathroom and kitchen being added. Land has been added to the property to create the lovely gardens.

It was from Holly Cottage that Hayton Bent's first taxi service was run before the 1939-45 war. Frank Winwood drove a taxi cab in Ludlow and Frank brought his taxi home to Holly Cottage; any one who needed to get to

Bill and Doug Friswell outside Holly Cottage in 1939

Ludlow early to catch a train could hire Frank to take them down. Taxis were then mostly used by people who were better off, but most people walked, unable or unwilling to pay the modest taxi fare. The Winwood family moved from Holly Cottage to live in Ludlow on May 1st 1939, thus bringing to an end Hayton's one and only official taxi service!

The next dwelling along Chapel Road is High Grove, a smallholding situated on the left hand side with a communal water pump at its entrance. Many dwellings got their drinking water from here before the arrival of the piped supply. The top of the pump now appears to be missing; it is a great pity that these old relics of parish life are being removed, or neglected. They do not belong to individual landowners, but were, and therefore still are, part and parcel of the community.

High Grove is now run as a riding stables, having an up to date stable block and an all-weather schooling yard attached. Up until 1948 Highgrove was Hayton Bent's post office, run by the Wadeley family. Joe Wadeley had been the postman making deliveries, whilst his wife was post-mistress. Mrs.Wadeley retired in 1948, and the post office then moved to Browns Corner.

It is not clear when Hayton first had its own post office, or postal deliveries, but the records the G.P.O. (General Post Office), show that stamped letters were only bound to be delivered free of any charge except for the postage as from 1863, but even this only initially covered cities and towns. By 1901 some 866 cities and towns were included in this scheme, but it would appear that rural populations had only received a free delivery service a few years earlier. From the 1881 records of the village of Stanton Lacy, we see that Arthur Bowskill is entered as 'School Master' and 'Postmaster', which suggests that a post office then existed in the village. Many post offices did exist in country villages, but one had to deliver outgoing letters to that office, and collect any incoming mail from there—and pay a duty on it. It was from 1896 that a free rural collection and delivery service was made available, and it is from this time that collecting boxes sprang up around the country roads and lanes.

The small field adjoining High Grove and running on to join the road at Hayton Bank on the east side is called Postmans Patch. This was once a resting place for the postman's pony on which he made his deliveries, and the postman had a rest hut behind the thick holly hedge in the corner opposite Pillar Box Farm. The G.P.O. paid rent for this small paddock, which had once been a wood, but had been felled for some reason—just like those opposite High Croft, mentioned in the chapter on Hayton Bank.

Perhaps one may be wondering why I am paying so much attention to the postal service, but I feel that it is important concerning the history of the next and last house on Chapel Road: Pillar Box Farm, which gains its name from the G.P.O. collection box that had been built into the gable end of the house. It is not possible that Pillar Box Farm is the original name of this dwelling, for the house dates from around 1830, so was in existence some 66 years before pillar boxes came into use in Hayton. In my childhood it was called The Corners by one and all.

Pillar Box Farm is now a smallholding and is home to a number of species of farm animals and birds that takes one back to the old days—the days when one would expect to see a wide range of farm animals and birds living together.

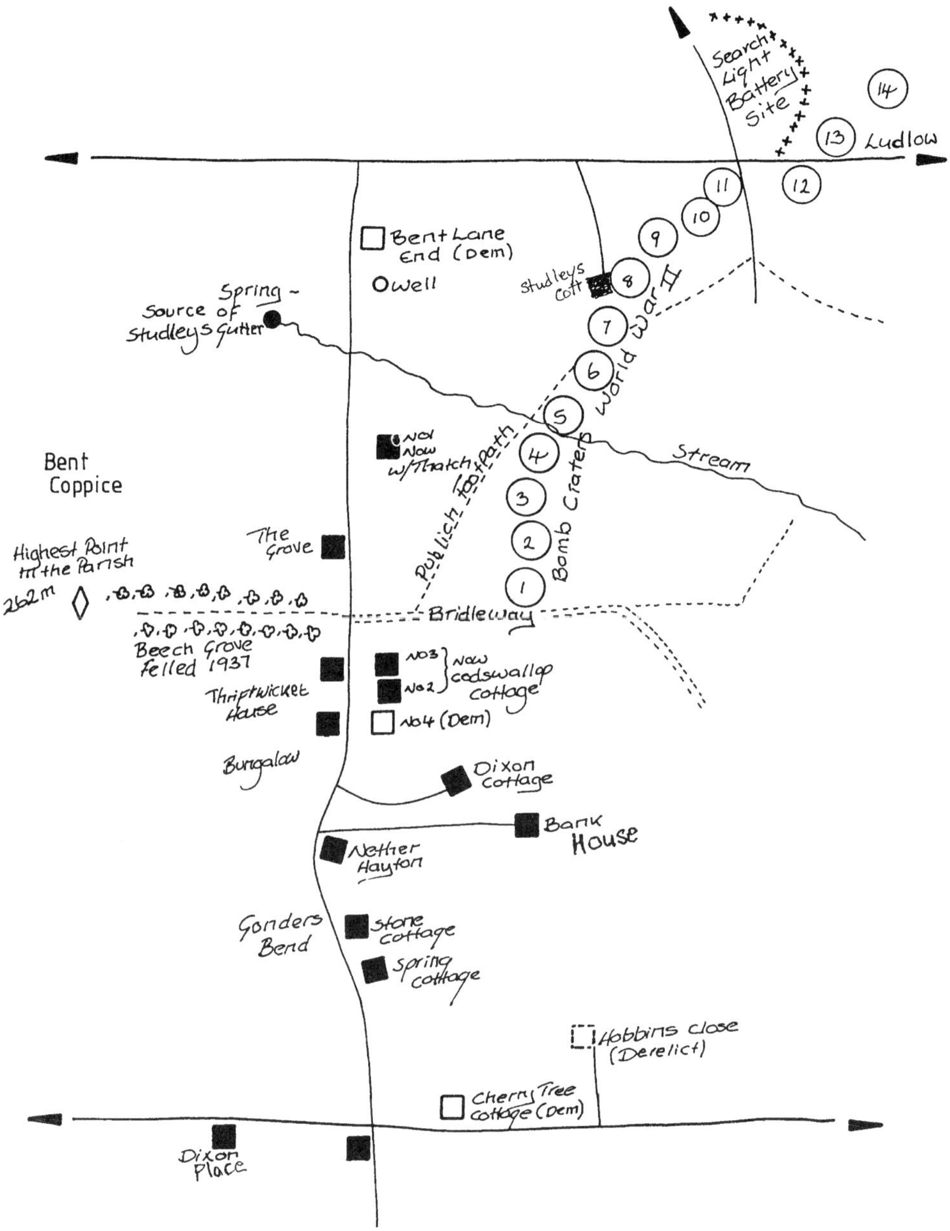

Map of Thriftwicket Lane

CHAPTER XX

Thriftwicket Lane

Retracing our steps from Pillar Box Farm and arriving back at the cross lanes, we turn left into Thriftwicket Lane. Any thoughts from the reader that we pass through a small gate thus entering a place of thrift, can be dismissed, for Thriftwicket Lane means nothing more than 'the lane to the Sorbus wood'. Thrift is derived from the Old English 'Fyrhthe' or 'Frith' meaning a wood. Wicket, Wicket tree leasow, Wicky tree, Witty tree leasow, The Witty tree, Witty are all associated with a place where the mountain ash (*sorbus aucuparia*) tree is, or was once growing. There is a 'Witty tree field', and a 'Witty tree bridge' in Stanton Lacy parish. The wood was once used in the whittling of small wooden objects, and hence the derivation. The mountain ash is in fact not the true Witty tree, which is a cross between two of the sorbus families. One fine old specimen is to be found in the Wyre Forest. Whitty Pear is a name often given to the fruits of the service tree, (*sorbus domestica*), which are edible when overripe.

Spring Cottage, Stone Cottage and Nether Hayton, are the first group of dwellings in Thriftwicket. They are huddled at the side of the lane on Gonders Bend, an incorrect pronunciation of Ganders Bend, a place to stop and view, as a male goose (gander) stops and looks, keeping watch over his family. In Shropshire the gander or male goose is called a 'gonder', hence Gonders Bend. Before the hedges became neglected on Hayton Bent, and before the hedgerow timber became mature, grand views of parts of the Corvedale could be seen from Gonders Bend.

The first cottage is Spring Cottage, once a double dwelling built in 1880, and it was from here that Hayton Bent had its first bus service, being the home of Frank Sadler, the driver.

Stone Cottage was also once a double dwelling. This cottage was demolished and an attractive stone cottage has been built on the old site.

Nether Hayton is the third dwelling, a large newly-built property which stands on the site of an old bothy, a barn with a fireplace used by shepherds or other workmen when working too far away to travel home. The name Nether Hayton is somewhat puzzling. Nether means the lowest part possible, the words lower and upper not being part of the English language before the 17th century. For upper the word 'Over' was used. Nether Hayton is situated on the 256 metre contour line, some 160 metres above the Nether! But everyone to their choice!

A drive at the side of Nether Hayton leads up to Bank House, a well built cottage in a lovely spot, with views of the hills beyond Corvedale. I consider this Bank House to be one of those dwellings that were built with monies borrowed from a bank. Many people named such dwelling with tongue in cheek.

Close by Bank House stands Dixon Cottage, the first home of the Rev. Lancelot Dixon, curate of the parish of Cold Weston, before he had Dixon Place built around 1830. My mother's family owned and lived here from the end of the First World War until 1921. Dixon Cottage has now been extended into quite a large dwelling.

The next dwelling on the lane is a sectional bungalow situated on the left hand side and is comparatively new.

Thriftwicket House is an old 'long-house'—a house with a farm building, usually a cow house, attached, and all existing under one continuous roof—and also stands on the left hand side. Shadrach Sankey, cobbler and cordwainer, once had a shop here. There are several cobblers and shoemakers listed over the years within the parish. A cobbler repaired boots and shoes, whilst a shoemaker made them, working only with new leather, and a cordwainer repaired or made other leather goods, such as horse harnesses, belts, and well buckets. Shadrach moved from Thriftwicket House between the censuses of 1871 and 1881, the latter showing him living in the Hope and now termed 'shoemaker'.

The Sankey family then lived in one of the thatched cottages situated in the small field opposite Hope Chapel. This cottage was demolished in the 1960s or 70s. Philip Keene is now owner occupier of Thriftwicket House, being born there, his father having bought the property from the Furber family in 1939.

Top Left: No.1 Thriftwicket Lane, now Wadboro Thatch. This cottage was built in 1687 by Richard Smout, the date carved into the main support beam. The property was recently sold as a 15th century cottage with its own ghost
Top Right: The Hayton Flyer with Nancy and Norman Keene. The desired speed was reached by kicking backwards with one foot, whilst the wheel hubs were filled with hard, unpalatable margarine, grease being scarce in the 1940s, hence 'the kickstart and margarine drive model'
Bottom Left: Mrs. V. Keene with evacuees
Bottom Right: Outdoors Barbers Shop. From the left: the late Andrew Smout, the late Cyril James, the late Arthur Keene, Mrs. V. Keene with son Norman. The barber is Bernard Sckoylas

Smouts and Walkers top left, Keenes top right
Bottom: The horse Kitty with Phil Keene closely watched by his father, Arthur, in his Home Guard uniform in 1943, whilst on the right Phil Keene is in best bib and tucker one year later

Top Left: Arthur Keene shearing a Clun ram

Top Right: Bringing the harvest home; Nellie James, Phil Keene and Cyril James with Arthur Keene loading

Centre Left: Pig killing at No.1 Thriftwicket Lane, 1949. From the left: Ian Jackson, Cyril James, Philip Keene, Dick Carter and unknown

Lower Left: Local transport in the 1940s. Various Keenes with George Nield at the rear of the horse

Over the lane from Thriftwicket House, there stood, until the 1970s, Nos.2, 3 and 4, Thriftwicket Lane, all three houses belonging to the Plymouth Estates. No.4 was demolished, whilst Nos.2 and 3 have been joined to make a single dwelling now named Codswallop Cottage. A communal well with its pump still *in situ* can be found in the field behind these old dwellings. My family lived at No.3 Thriftwicket Lane until 1966 having moved there from Rose Cottage, the Bullring, in 1934.

Moving on, we arrive at The Grove. The house has been extended and modernized recently, and now bears very little resemblance to the longhouse that stood here previously. The land has been taken from The Grove and is now farmed within a much larger unit. During my early childhood The Grove was a small dairy farm, the occupant one William Henner who ran a Ludlow milk round from here.

From the stile on the public footpath taking us from Thriftwicket Lane to Bent Coppice, there ran until the late 1930s a grove of beech trees. This grove measured 8 metres wide and ran to the highest point of Stanton Lacy Parish (OS 523804) situated just outside the confines of Bent Coppice. The point has now been eroded, and is not as conspicuous as it once was, but had previously been built up as a point on which to stand to gain a 360 degree view over the Bent so as to see see where one's stock was grazing. The Methodists once held their outdoor meeting at 'the point', probably before any of their present chapels were built. In later years, the point became a meeting place in summer for the local young men, who were often joined on warm summer evenings by the servant girls from Downton Hall on their days off.

The beech grove was felled in 1937 and the wire fence which parted the grove from the field was removed. Evidence of this beech grove can still be seen, the butt plates took years to rot away and the depressions where they stood are still in evidence. It is said that Grove House got its name from this lovely old beech grove.

Englishes Wood ran around the edge of Shortwood and Hayton Bent Commons, more or less following the lines of Studleys Gutter. It is not clear from the old maps if Englishes Wood joined up with Bent Coppice, but it would appear that there was a wood or a coppice situated on the lane, hence Thriftwicket. There are mountain ash trees in the hedges leading to Bent Coppice, and within the coppice, Studleys Gutter also has its share of mountain ash;apart from these three sites, very few mountain ash 'Whitty trees' are to be found locally.

From The Grove cottage, the lane changes its name, becoming Bent Lane. The lane is now overgrown, but before much of Hayton Bent became a neglected area, the hedges were brashed each year, (i.e. cut by hand with a brashing hook), and the lane from hedge to hedge was covered in white clover. The Keene family, the Teague family of The Grove, and the Martins family of No.1, grazed their cattle on the lane during spring and summer. No.1 Thriftwicket Lane, (the area is known as Thriftwicket for postal reasons only), has been renovated into a comfortable dwelling, but still retains its thatched roof, the property now being called Wadboro Thatch. No.1 was offered for sale by the Plymouth Estates to a sitting tenant for £150 in the 1960s. This offer was turned down, £150 being thought to be too high a price for the house and three acres of land. It was recently on the market for £145,000.

No evidence of the last dwelling on Bent Lane can now be found, but Bent Lane End stood on the right hand side of the lane just beyond the spring which forms the source of Studleys Gutter. Most of this dwelling was knocked, or fell, down in the first part of the present century, but until the 1960s some stone and brick work remained hidden in a thicket of blackthorn. A feature of this property was its very deep well, covered only with a wooden door. As kids we often removed the door to drop bricks and stones into the well. The water level never appeared to change, there being a drop of some 12 ft. of dry well before the water level. However, it was difficult to get at any water, as the winding gear had fallen, or had been thrown, down the well, making it almost impossible to get past with a bucket.

Gypsies who camped in the mouth of Bent Lane for a couple of weeks each year used the well for their source of drinking water for both themselves and their horses. These gypsies stayed here whilst they made clothes pegs, the women hawking them around from door to door, selling and begging as they went. I often stopped to watch the menfolk whittle the hazel wands into pegs, while another man cut tin cans into thin strips to fix the heads of the pegs together. This was clever and interesting work to a small boy, far better than chanting tables in the school room.

We have now reached the 'Top Road' and must retrace our steps back to Chapel Road.

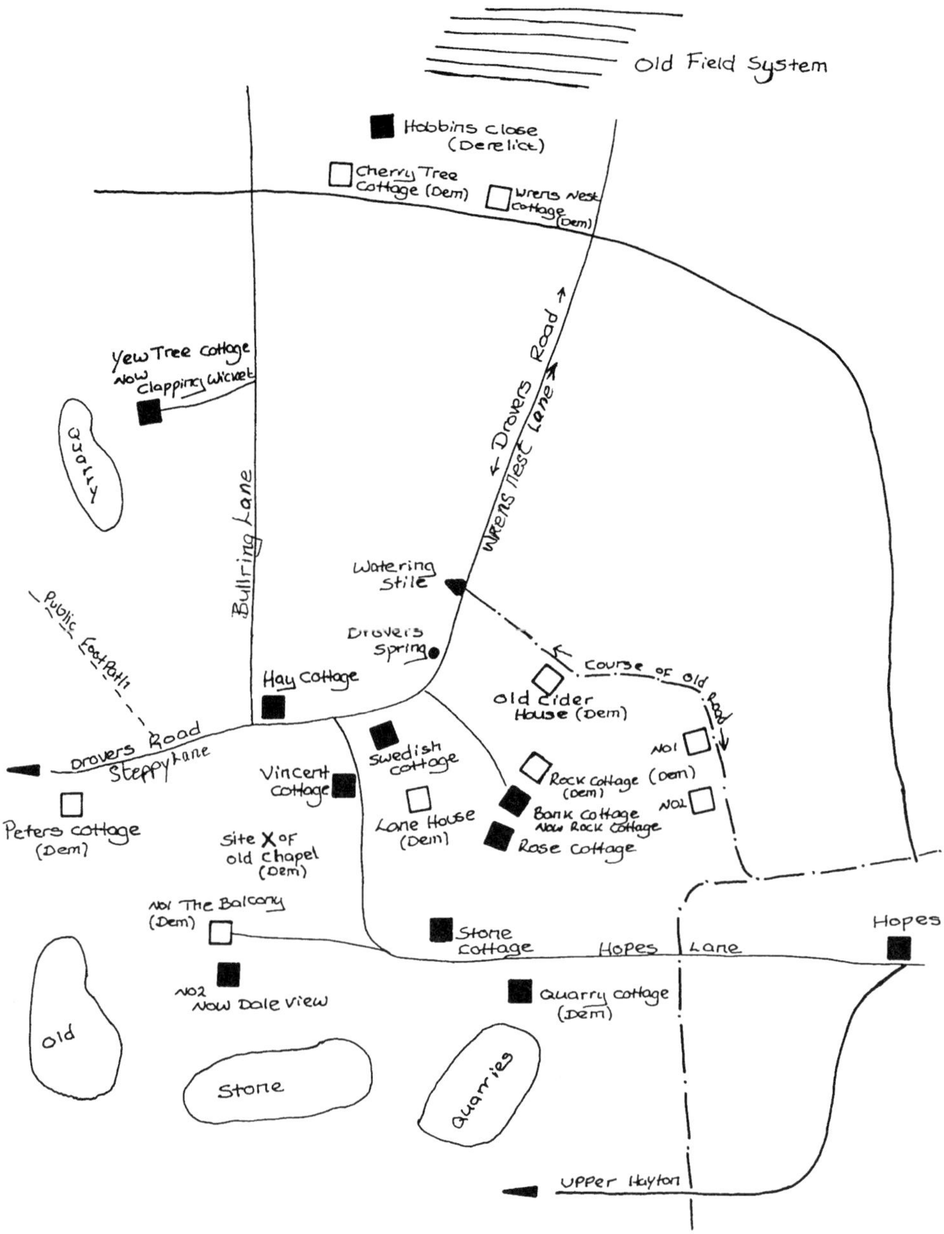

Map of The Bullring

CHAPTER XXI

The Bullring

The Bullring, once the market place, is situated on what was then the main Ludlow road and must have been a busy place some 300 years ago. Five roads lead to The Bullring, three of which are still used, whilst the other two have only become disused this century, these being the Old Titterhill Lane and Hopes Lane.

Two unofficial names have been given to The Bullring over the years. One was The Kingdom, so called because the Smout families occupied all dwellings except the Yew Tree at one time, the other was Little Brummigum (Birmingham), because during the war years every dwelling excepting Dale View Cottage was occupied by families from Birmingham. My Great Uncle Tom stuck it out at Dale View Cottage until his death in 1952.

There were a further eight cottages, and a chapel in The Bullring some 200 years ago, and the sites of all of these can still be traced if one cares to look closely.

We will approach The Bullring down the only metalled road, Bullring Lane. The first cottage, situated on the right hand side, is now called Clapping Wicket Cottage, an old stone cottage that has been renovated into a comfortable home, but is still without its ‘Clapping Wicket’. (A clapping wicket was a gate which closed by the use of a weight, the gate making a ‘clapping’ noise as it swung back against the post, it often bouncing back to only close at the fifth strike. Such gates were used to give warning to the occupier of someone approaching.) The cottage was formerly Yew Tree Cottage. The land from Bullring Lane to Hayton Bank, small fields comprising some 24 acres, were farmed from the Yew Tree until 1930. But this was not the case in 1848 when the Tithe Commissioners Map lists the dwelling as:-

Plot 163, being a cottage and garden, 3 rods, 5 perches
Owner: Earl of Craven
Tenant: John Griffiths

The Tithe of 2/6d was payable to the Vicar. The same map refers to the land in question as allotments, ridge and furrow are still in evidence, from this we gather that the fields were worked as a communal holding by the occupants of the Bullring.

The owner occupiers of Clapping Wicket Cottage have given a home to two donkeys from The Donkey Sanctuary. Jack and Ned now have a comfortable happy home, and are of great interest to the local children.

Hay Cottage, is the next dwelling on the lane, at the junction with Steppy Lane. Hay Cottage was once a double dwelling. The last two families to live in the double dwelling were the families of Richard and William Smout, who moved from here in 1927 after a fire had destroyed the interior of the building. The property stood derelict from 1927 until the 1970s when it was renovated into a modern home. The Tithe Commissioners Map, 1848, record reads:

House and garden
Owner: Richard Edwards
Tenant: Richard Edwards

This Richard Edwards had married one Margaret Smout, who would have been my great great aunt. It is from her that my great uncles Dick and Bill Smout inherited the property

Hay Cottage is shown as Parcel 159 on the Tithe Map, Hay Cottage being a recent name, the total land being shown as '1 rod, 9 perches'. The paddock now included within the confines of the property was then shown as a separate holding:

Parcel 160, Enclosure on Hayton
1 acre (Arable)
Owner Richard Hall
Tenant Thomas Everall

Tithes payable were 6d. to the Vicar, 2/- to William Hall, and 1/10d to the J.E. Graham Trustees. This total sum of 4/4d on one acre seems to have been a high price to pay back in the 1840s.

Part of Corvedale from the Bullring

This small one acre paddock now has some 97 different species of wild flowers and grasses growing on it, proving that wild flowers will return to an area if left unploughed for many years.

Turning right handed into Steppy Lane, a public footpath stile is on the right. This footpath runs out onto Hayton Bank by the Old Methodist Chapel, whilst another branch runs up the steep field leading on to Hayton Bank just below the Linney. The first two fields are part of the old allotment system, the ridge and furrow are plain to see. At the end of the second field is the old 'clay-plain' running from the public footpath back to Steppy Lane. Soil was dug from this plain and taken to build up the 'wheat terraces' that can be seen on our left as we enter the third field. Wheat was planted by hand on a terrace, one yard wide, which was formed by drawing the soil into rows about 4 inches high, the spaces between the terraces being left for drainage. A field would contain several such terraces, each family in the community cultivating one or more terrace. These terraces are now bracken covered, but it is still possible to identify them. All these small fields are known locally as the Chapel Fields and are home to many flowers and plants. A 1995 survey by English Nature and myself turned up 119 different species.

Returning to Steppy Lane, some 50 metres further on from the stile and situated in the orchard to the left can be seen the old house platform of the Pelers Cottage, together with a few stones marking the wall that parted the property from the lane. The better stone was taken for building elsewhere, whilst the inferior stuff was put in the foundations of the Bullring Lane when the first attempt at metalling was carried out in the late 1940s. The cottage's name derives from 'Pel', Old English for the fleece of a dead sheep. The wool was plucked out by a person known as the peler, was then washed, cleaned and spun by the peler, or by anyone with a spinning wheel.

Parcel 157 on the 1848 Tithe Map, I consider to refer to the old Pelers Cottage:

> Cottage and garden
> Owner: Benjamin Breakwell

Each drovers' road had its 'peler'. They would deal with any dead sheep who died upon the drovers' road, burying or disposing of the carcass in exchange for the wool. Local farmers also got rid of dead sheep by courtesy of the 'peler'. Many of these old 'peler cottages' have had their names changed or misspelt by people who do not understand the old ways, but in the neighbouring parish of Stoke St. Milborough, we still find a small farm with the delightful name of Pel Begger Farm situated on another of the old drovers' roads.

Sadly, in Munslow Parish remains of the old cottage still stand at the side of the old road, but the area is now called 'The Speller' instead of 'The Peler': it would appear that many people locally cannot refer to anything without adding an 's' or two. For example within our Parish, Hayton Bent has become Hayton's Bent, Hopton Gate is now Hopton's Gate, and Rock Green, once in Stanton Lacy Parish, is now referred to as Rock's Green.

With the coming of the railways, and there being an improved toll road system from 1811, the practice of driving animals great distances, such as from north Shropshire to south Wales, from Shropshire to Liverpool and on to Ireland by ferry, or from the North to London, came to an end, although the old drovers roads were again used briefly during the two World Wars, there then being no transport available for the transporting of livestock to and from the markets.

The old drovers' roads can still be identified by such places as Peler, Taffy's Piece, Paddy's Ground, Welshmans, Ireland, or Little London, names derived from the areas where different bands of drovers camped overnight. There would have been pounds close by where the stock could be shut in during the night, such places usually had a pub or a cider house close by.

Opposite Hay Cottage lies Vincent Cottage, not shown in the 1848 survey as the house was built in 1863, on the old market place. The market itself is thought to have ceased as such around 1810 due to the toll road system, and perhaps the lack of water within this area for it is recorded that the local water courses dried up for some unknown reason in the infant years of the 19th century. The local stocks were also said to have been in position on the market place. Those poor unfortunate girls from the Lydehole would have been placed in the stocks here.

On the 1848 Tithe Map, the plot now holding Vincent Cottage was entered as:-

Plot 158, Close with Chapel
2 rods and 15 perches (Arable)
Owner: Vincent Hardwick
Tenant: Vincent Hardwick

Tithes of £1 0s 1d were payable to William Hall and 1s. to the J.E. Graham Trustees. Again, £1 1s 1d seems a high price to pay for such a small parcel of land.

There is no mention of the chapel in the records excepting those recording it. We can however look upon this building as being Hayton Bent's first chapel, giving one a pointer to how important The Bullring was in those days, especially with the market place standing at the side of what was then the main Ludlow Road from this area.

The Methodist Movement really took off in this part of the country around 1781. The Wesleyan Movement which itself spawned the Methodist Movement in 1812, really took off around 1812. We can be more or less certain that The Bullring chapel was a Wesleyan one; the Anglican Church has not recorded it, so we can also be certain that it was nothing to do with them. Additionally the records mention no 'Tithe' payable to the vicar from this property.

Vincent Hardwick built himself a cottage on Plot 158 in 1863, many years after this chapel had been made redundant, and fourteen years after the Victorian job had been built on Hayton Bank. The Wesleyan Chapel on Chapel Road had been built in 1830, this one probably replacing The Bullring Chapel!

If you turn right into Hopes Lane, the entrance to Vincent Cottage lies on the right, opposite which is the old entrance to Rose Cottage garden, where the remains of the wicket gate can still be seen. A path led from this gate through the garden, then down a flight of steps to Rose Cottage, much the same as the entrance to Stone Cottage further on down the lane.

The entrance and garden of Rose Cottage now holds a wooden bungalow named Swedish Cottage whose grounds also include the garden and site of Lane Cottage. The 1848 Tithe Map records Lane Cottage as:

Plot 154, Cottage and garden
1 rod 24 perches
Owner: Earl of Craven
Tenant: Ann Lloyd

Three years later, in the census of 1851, we find that the said Ann Lloyd had gathered her family around her:

Plot 153		
Naomi Simokes	38	Charwoman
Cunnery Simokes	14	Agricultural labourer
John Simokes	10	
Ann Lloyd	76	Pauper - Mother
Edwin Lloyd	5	Pauper - Nephew
William Simokes	81	Pauper Mason - Uncle

What a vulgar word pauper is. Anyone who lived on parish relief was termed a pauper, even a child of five years old. There being no pension schemes in those days, one worked until work became impossible and then became a pauper. Perhaps us present day pensioners should be termed 'Pauper Pensioners'.

One may be thinking what a strange name 'Simokes' is! It is in fact an incorrect spelling of 'Simkiss', who were related to my family.

Thomas Smout bought several properties on The Bullring around 1860. These included Rock Cottage, Rose Cottage, Lane Cottage, Balcony Cottage and Quarry Cottage. Other properties were in the hands of his relatives, Hay Cottage being owned by his brother-in-law, Richard Edwards, who had also owned Balcony Cottage and its neighbour, (plot 156). Thomas Smout II sold plot 153 with its derelict house and garden, plus Rose Cottage garden to Edith Chapman of Vincent Cottage in 1948 for the grand sum of £40.

The next dwelling on the left is Stone Cottage, now a much enlarged and improved dwelling, like all its Bullring neighbours. From the map of 1848 we see it is listed as:

Plot 155 Cottage and Garden
1 rod 8 perches
Owner: Vincent Hardwick
Tenant: Vincent Hardwick

Tithe payable to the Vicar was 1d. Vincent Hardwick is the same Hardwick who had Vincent Cottage built.

My great grandparents owned and lived at Stone Cottage, 'Stallion George' living on there until his death in 1948. Stallion George Smout got this somewhat unusual name, not from any sexual notoriety, but from his trade in horse flesh. George lead his Shire stallions around the farms to serve the mares; he also dressed and prepared horses for shows and fairs.

My great grandfather Francis Smout died at Stone Cottage in 1926. Rhesa Evison 'Carpenter and Coffin maker' of Stanton Lacy was contracted to make a coffin of elm for great grandfather. It was the practice in those days for the corpse to lie at home until the coffin was made and the day of the funeral arrived, when the coffin was taken to the house, the corpse placed in, the lid screwed down, whence it was taken straight to the church in time for the funeral, but in Francis Smout's case this was not to be. Here I will quote Rhesa Evison:

My great grandmother aged 92 at Stone Cottage in 1929

> There was a thick snow lying that had frozen on top. I sez to owd Chris we 'ud better go an' fetch owd Frank down a bit closer to the church, this being the day before the funeral; we often did this in bad weather. We 'ud let 'em lie in the shop overnight, with the doors locked o' course! We harnessed the owd mare into a flat bottom cyart, an' sets off fer Hayton. We got as far as the Hopes. I sez to Chris 'I dunna think we shall make it up the Bank in this, we 'ud better walk up over the Balcony and carry 'im down.'

We struggled up Balcony Bank 'aving left the hoss an cyart at the Hopes. At every step we broke through the frozen crust an' went in up to our knees, but in the end, we got there, explaining to Mrs. Smout what we intended doing. 'Er agreed. We gets owd Frank in an' screws him down, an' struggles back towards the Hopes. When we 'ud gone 50 yards, an' was out o' sight of anyone from the 'ouse, we drops the coffin down. 'We be never goin' to get owd Frank down to the Hopes this way.' Sez I, 'We 'ull never make it!'

Sorting through our pockets we both produced some thin cord, brought for the purpose. We ties some to the coffin handles and lets it slide gently over the snow. Now as ya knows, we was both getting on in years, an' was nowhere near as nimble as a once was. As we gets into the last field, we begins to gather speed. Owd Chris goes flat on 'is face, losing go 'is cord. The box spins around, throwing me arse over yud. I too looses go, now there's owd Frank speeding over the snow out of control. We struggles after 'im, but luck was with us, as the field levelled out, the coffin more or less stops and we catches 'er up. There be no damage done, but I ull tell thee what chap! Owd Frank 'ad got me frit! An I 'ull tell thee summat else: Owd Frank was travelling smartish for a 'jud 'un' as we approached the Hopes.

My great uncle 'Stallion George'

Over the way from Stone Cottage is Dale View Cottage, once Balcony Cottages, there being two properties here. The map of 1848 lists them as:

Parcel 156, 2 cottages with gardens
1 rod and 20 perches

Here we see that it was owned by my great great uncle, Richard Edwards. The tenants were John Jones and Richard Davies. No.1 The Balcony must have become ruinous in the last quarter of the 19th century, for it was a tumbled down ruin by the time my father was born at Rock Cottage in 1896. The site on which No.1 stood now holds the garage for No.2 The Balcony, now named Dale View Cottage. This dwelling is now a much improved cottage, with wonderful views of the Corvedale from both house and gardens.

Just below Stone Cottage, on the opposite side of Hopes Lane, once stood Quarry Cottage. Evidence of the house platform and the garden hedges are still visible. This cottage, like others in the parish was probably ruinous before the Tithe Commissioners Map came into being, although part of this building was still standing in the early 1930s.

Hopes Lane ran from The Bullring down between Stone Cottage and Dale View Cottage, the Ordnance Survey maps now showing a public footpath over part of its course. The lane ran down the side of Balcony Bank and on down to the old public house, The Hopes. It was crossed at the bottom of Balcony Bank by the old lane from Titterhill Quarry to Upper Hayton. The lane hedges were grubbed out around 1947, but if one looks, one can still pick out the line of the hedges.

Returning to the junction of The Bullring and Hopes Lanes, we turn into that part of the old Ludlow Road known locally as Wrens Nest Lane, which leads us from The Bullring to Titterhill Lane, or Woodlands Road, as it is now called. Opposite to the plot that holds Swedish Cottage, lies the small paddock which now forms part of Hay Cottage's property. Near the gate at lane side there was once a small pool which has now silted up, causing the water from the spring that fed it to run down the lane thus spoiling its surface.

My father remembered there being oak posts complete with tethering chains, situated in this paddock next to the lane when he was a small boy around 1900. These may have been chains for tethering bulls, but I can find no real records of The Bullring. The 1848 Tithe Map came too late to record its early history. I am only able to write what has been passed down through family history, but I believe that my account is a true account, so far as it has been possible to prove!

A path on the right leads down to two cottages. There were once three cottages here, Rock Cottage, Bank Cottage and Rose Cottage. Rock Cottage was demolished around 1870; it stood close to Bank Cottage in the corner of the field on the left. The garden of Rock Cottage ran up to the Wrens Nest Lane, the garages of the present Rock Cottage and Rose Cottage now stand on the top end of it.

Thomas Smout I bought Rock Cottage, Bank Cottage and Rose Cottage in 1862. Rock Cottage was already a ruin at this time, but it remained in the

My mother, Emily Smout

family until 1944 when Thomas Smout II sold the ruin and garden to Mrs. Wilkes of Rock Cottage for the sum of £10. I must explain here that the title deeds to the property now known as Rock Cottage prove that until the late 19th century it was Bank Cottage, the name Rock Cottage being taken over after the original Rock Cottage had become ruinous.

Rock Cottage has once again been taken over by the Smout family, my wife Hazel and I having bought the property in 1993. Apart from having a bathroom, utility room and a kitchen extension added, the property remains much as it must have been when my grandmother was born here in 1874, but sadly its orchards, that ran down to the bottom of Balcony Bank, were sold to the neighbouring farmer by the previous owner, and have now disappeared into the adjoining field.

Next to Rock Cottage stands Rose Cottage, and it was here that I was born in the early 1930s, moving to Thriftwicket Lane early in 1934. Mother and father had moved into Rose Cottage after their marriage in 1927, father having been granted the tenancy by his Aunt Fanny. She had taken over several houses on The Bullring due to her second husband, Clemson Westwood, purchasing the properties from Thomas Smout II, Fanny's brother.

Fanny Westwood, my great aunt, had lost her first husband in the 1914-1918 war. Her second husband was a businessman from Wolverhampton who had no time for The Bullring, or its inhabitants, and convinced Aunt Fan that there was nothing to be gained out of Rock and Rose Cottages. She sold both properties in 1928 to the local butcher, Harry Bengry, of The Grove, Thriftwicket Lane. Harry bought Rock Cottage and Rose Cottage, together with with the garden and orchards of Rock Cottage for £55. Thomas Smout had held on to the garden of Rose Cottage for some reason.

Father was enraged at the selling of the family property. With a young family he could not afford to buy it himself. The new owner wanted us out as he had plans for the properties which did not include us, so father got Rose Cottage condemned as being unfit for human habitation. This meant that the owner could not charge rent on the property until the property was brought up to a certain standard, but Harry would not do any repairs whilst we were still living there. Stalemate resulted until May 1934 when my parents finally gave in and moved to Thriftwicket Lane. Harry's plans for Rose Cottage had by then grown cold. Families came to live in Rose Cottage during the war years, being allowed to live in the condemned property, but the owners still not being allowed to charge any rent.

After the war the cottage remained condemned until it was modernized in the late 1970s. A wing was built on, the owner, who also owned Rock Cottage at that time, took part of Rock Cottage garden to form a garden at Rose Cottage, at the same time an access on foot was granted over Rock Cottage property to Rose Cottage.

Continuing on down Wrens Nest Lane, on the left hand side there is what remains of the old drovers' spring, where the drovers and travellers using the Ludlow road could obtain clear spring water until early in the 19th century, when the spring all but dried up. A land drain has now been laid into the area of the spring, resulting in a flush of water during a wet period.

All that remains of the drovers' spring, into which a land drain has now been laid

Below the drovers' spring, and on the same side, we see the watering stile, though a wire fence erected at the side of the lane blocks the entrance. The watering stile was still open to the lane until the 1930s, whilst a hedge separated it from the surrounding fields. Evidence of the boundary hedges can still be seen.

The remains of the watering stile, now forming part of the field

Opposite the entrance to the watering stile, the mouth of the Old Titterhill Lane is marked by the two oak gateposts that once held the oak gate to the lane that ran down to the Cider House, The Pound and Patch. The Cider House was situated some 80 metres down the field, the remains of the dwelling being finally cleared away around the mid 1960s, when the small fields which had once formed the pounds were incorporated into one large field. At the same time, the small brook that carried the overflow from the watering stile, and which also took the surface water from the lane, was filled in and piped. This was not a great success! During wet weather the stream still follows its old course on the outside of the land drain pipe system.

From the old Cider House, Titterhill Lane followed and formed the boundary between those lands which were farmed from Potters Farm, and Titterhill Cottage. This lane is still in evidence on the ground throughout its entire length! On the lower side of the lane, and in the old orchard known locally for generations as 'Watkins Orchard' the remains of two old dwellings can be seen, their platforms marked by huge stones. The old lane forked just beyond these cottages, the left hand fork leading up to Titterhill Quarry, the

A stretch of the old Titterhill Lane which ran from the Bullring to Titterhill Cottage

right hand fork down to the bottom of the steep bank where it once again forked, one branch leading out on to Titterhill close to Titterhill Cottage, the other fork running right handed down the side of the Hopes Meadow and along the bottom of Balcony Bank. Having crossed over Hopes Lane, it then ran on to join the Lower Hayton to Upper Hayton road between the White House and Sinks Corner.

Returning to the watering stile, if you carry on up Wrens nest Lane, on the left hand side it is plain to see the old raised walkway where the travellers and drovers walked, the stock walking in the bottom of the lane. Arriving at Titterhill Road, or Woodlands Road, as it is now called, we end our journey over The Bullring.

CHAPTER XXII

Transport & Deliveries

Being situated close to a main road, the village of Stanton Lacy enjoyed the privilege of public transport several years before the rest of the parish. In the 1920s a bus service was running down what is now the B4365. Freemans and Owens bus services were also operating from Munslow, running along the Peaton Ludlow road. It has not been possible to find the exact year, but it is thought that these services were in operation by 1920.

In the census of 1881, horse drawn carriers service were operated by John Evison from Stanton Lacy to Ludlow and back on Mondays only, and Eliza Brooks from Lower Hayton to Ludlow and back every Monday and Saturday. Hayton Bent was served by Mrs. Massey of Clee St. Margaret, who ran services along the Top Road every Monday and Friday.

All these horse drawn carrier carts as they were termed, served much as the later bus service did, but were only used by a few people of the parishes; many people preferred to walk, whilst others with a pony and trap, pony and float, or cycle, were independent.

Hayton Bent had its first bus service in 1936, when Smiths Bus Service started operating from Ludlow. The local driver was Frank Sadler, living at Spring Cottage, Thriftwicket Lane. Frank brought his single axled 20 seater home with him each evening and operated from home on local runs. Sometimes the old bus played up and would not start, or decided that the Hope or Hayton Bank was too much for it. On these occasions, Frank would turn her round and reverse up, reverse being a lower gear than bottom, but on a few occasions, the old girl would refuse even in reverse gear: 'I will have to ask all the young people to walk up!' Frank would shout, and all under 30 years old would do so. Some young women, no more than 25 years old would sink deeper into their seats, trying to look older than their years, to save having to walk. Others who had children now grown up would nip off the bus and walk, thus trying to pretend that they were much younger than their true age.

Even when everything was going well, the journey to Ludlow was often a long drawn out affair. Frank would bring the bus to a halt by some farm gate. 'I wonder if Mrs. So and So is comin' toda? 'Er come uve us last wik. I 'ull jest gi' 'er a minute or two.' Sometimes Mrs. So and So would put in an appearance, sometimes the waiting was in vain. With this slapdash attitude a bus timetable was useless and a crystal ball was just as accurate, but the service was a godsend to the women and children, however unreliable it may seem to have been. Not many men travelled on the bus in early days terming it the 'canting cyart' and in the main left it strictly alone.

In the late 1930s, Greens Transport ran a bus service along the top road to Clee St. Margaret, but using the Hopton route from the Smithy.

Local Deliveries

Marston Brothers, bakers and confectioners, of Ludlow delivered twice weekly around the parish. Dick Weaver drove his horse drawn covered bakers van up till 1940 every Tuesday and Friday. His white horse was also named Dick. After 1940 he made his deliveries in a Ford 10 van.

Another firm of bakers and confectioners from Ludlow, Waits, also delivered twice weekly, every Monday and Thursday. Davis and Brown delivered every Wednesday, whilst Valentines also delivered once a week, as did the Co-op.

Pearce's Cake Shop made a delivery of 'fresh fancy cakes' every Thursday. Eric Butcher rode a cycle to which was attached a box like sidecar mounted on pram wheels. The box was fitted with shelves onto which the trays of cakes slotted. Eric cycled around the parish calling at each house trying to sell cakes. Over the fields and rough lanes he walked, having made up a selection of cakes on a tray and parked his bike. Eric had no lock on his sidecar and he would often return to his transport to find that cakes were missing. It was too big a temptation for hungry lads to resist.

I once filled my cap with cakes before running to a quiet spot to consume them. The jam tarts and lemon curd tarts were generously filled in those days, and arriving home I could not remove my cap; surplus curd and jam had stuck it firmly to my hair. Mother removed the cap with the aid of scissors, put two and two together, and a sound thrashing was my reward. I made a solemn promise never to do this again. The next week I was pleased to see that Eric's sidecar was sporting a brand new padlock, thus dismissing all temptation.

Watkins, butchers of Ludlow, delivered fresh meat every Friday, their transport being pony and float up to the outbreak of war, after which all deliveries were motorized due to most young men having been conscripted, or having volunteered for the armed services, leaving fewer men on whom to depend. A small van could, with one driver, cover as much distance in a week as four horsedrawn vans. Carpenters, butchers of Ludlow, also delivered meat by pony and float.

The *Ludlow Advertizer* and *Wellington Journal*, were delivered each Friday by Norman Jones from Ludlow who cycled around the parish. The Sunday papers were delivered by one Andrew Spruce, also by cycle.

International Stores, Guius Smiths and Gatehouse Stores all made weekly deliveries. Early in the week their runners would cycle round the parish to take people's orders. These were then made up and delivered on Fridays by horsedrawn vans until about 1940, after this by motorized transport, although the deliveries were discontinued by some stores.

Fresh fish was delivered each Friday. Rowland, who lived at No.3 Peewit Hall, drove around on a motorcycle with a home made attachment fitted in which to carry the boxes of fish. These were delivered from Grimsby to Ludlow railway station by express train—or so we were informed, but Rowland's fish were dry and dull-eyed by the time he called at the door. On frequent occasions the fish would spend the whole day in their boxes parked outside the New Inn, departing customers often helping themselves to what they fancied from the boxes, with Rowland too far gone to prevent them.

However, Rowland did have good kippers, properly cured and salted, a far cry from the orange dyed samples we get these days.

Postal Deliveries

Mail was fetched from Bromfield Railway Station six mornings a week, either by horse or on foot. It was sorted at Stanton Lacy Post Office, and then delivered on pony or foot or cycle, to the outlying areas of the parish as from 1896.

Joe Wadley was the first postman that I remember. He lived at High Grove, Hayton Bent, that being our local post office until 1949, and delivered the post on horseback.

Sammy Middleton, living opposite Hope Chapel in one of the cottages that were demolished in the 1970s, took over from Joe. Having no horse or cycle, Sammy walked. His day began at 6.30a.m. when he walked from the Hope to Stanton Lacy to collect the mail, he then delivered up the Hope, Downton Hall, Shortwood, Hopton Gate, Thriftwicket Lane, Bullring, The Woodlands, Titterhill, and thence along Chapel Road to High Grove.

The postman's rest hut stood in the corner of the small field opposite Pillar Box Farm. Here the postmen could find shelter in bad weather until the time when he could collect the mail from the box and begin his return journey. At the set time Sammy would empty the box then situated in the wall of the house, then walk over to the top of the Hope, then to Downton Hall, back to the box at the bottom of Hope, emptying the boxes as he went, taking the collections down to Stanton Lacy Post Office where they were sorted into different bags before being taken to Bromfield, and put on the mail trains. Sammy would then walk back up the Hope to his cottage. With today's junk mail this task would be an impossible one.

George Byetheway cycled from Clee St. Margaret to deliver mail at Bouldon, Peaton, Sutton, Sutton Hill, Lawton, Sutton Court, The Lyde Hole, Lower Hayton, Upper Hayton, Hayton Bank as far as the 'rest hut', he then cleared the boxes at Upper Hayton, Lower Hayton, Sutton Court, Peaton and Bouldon in the evenings. The G.P.O. had positioned another rest hut along the Peaton Road, just over the parish boundary at Elford Gate. This hut is still in its original place, being used as a store after the decline of the postal delivery on foot. George progressed to be a clock and watch repairer, which he carried out in the rest huts while waiting for the hour to arrive when he could clear the boxes and start for home. But those who trusted their timepieces to George were always in for a disappointment. Taken to task over the length of time a clock had been in his care, George would say: 'Dang me Missus, if I anna dropped the spring out on 'er, and it bin sa dark in the owd 'ut I conna put me 'and on 'er, but I'll find the bugger when the light gets a bit better, and you shall 'ave 'er back pretty smartish.' If a clock or watch was returned it would be soaked in paraffin with the dial discoloured. 'Ly 'er on 'er back fer a wik!' Or: 'Put 'er face down till the new part 'ave lossened up!' Instructed George.

Dad looked at our clock that had just been returned by George and said: 'Well, the bugger will tell the right time twice a day!' As a small boy I wondered about this statement, but in the end realized that this is true of any timepiece when stopped.

The District Nurse

Mrs. Downes, our local District Nurse, lived at Woodlands Farm where her husband, Richard, was the tenant farmer under the Plymouth Estates. Her transport was a pony and trap, or cycle. She knew all her patients, (mostly pregnant mothers), well and seemed to have that knack of knowing exactly when the baby would arrive. Husbands would send someone to fetch the nurse from the Woodlands in the middle of the night, saying 'the baby's coming'. These messengers often became infuriated by the nurse's lack of urgency as she packed her bag, making sure that all she needed was packed, but despite her apparent lack of speed, she always arrived in time.

With there being no telephone at Woodlands Farm, the Downes decided to move back to Bromfield where a telephone was available, making the nurse's job more bearable.

Pig Killing

Before the 1939-45 war, everyone kept and killed at least one pig a year, bacon being the staple diet; butchers meat could only be afforded for Sundays.

Nothing was wasted from the pig, even the ears were boiled. The bladders were dried and blown up with a hollow nettle stalk to make a football. Of course, being so light this was never very successful, and at the sight of a thorn, they were punctured!

The act of killing a pig some 60 years past was nothing short of a brutal act. The pig was hauled from its sty by strong men, lifted onto a bench, turned on its back and held down while its throat was cut. Its legs were then pumped furiously to make sure that the last drops of blood were drained from the body; the bacon would turn bad if any blood was left in the veins.

Tory George, from the 'Gold Coast' was our local pig killer. After the pig was dead, its body was scalded with boiling water, which softened up the bristles so that they were easy to scrape off. The pig was then hoisted up by its back legs, split open and the internal organs removed. The small and large intestines together with the stomach were washed and cleaned, soaked for nine days with a change of water each day, and then boiled on the ninth day: these were the chitterlings and were prized by the old folk, some butchers still sell chitterlings at around £3 per lb.

Meanwhile the pig's carcass was left to hang for 24 hrs, when the butcher returned to cut it up. The hams and flitches were salted down for bacon, the rest was turned into pork joints, fry, pork pies, and black puddings, whilst the fat was rendered down to make home cured lard. The dried bits left over from the rendering were the scratchings; today's pork scratchings are nothing but dried up hog rind, bearing no resemblance to the original scratchings. I once opened a packet in a Corvedale pub, the largest scratching in the packet was a complete sow's teat, I have never eaten these modern day scratchings since!

Some of the better off farmers would not bother with the 'belly' as the intestines were called, but would give them away to anyone who they considered would benefit most from them. The 'pig killer' would leave a bit of the fat on the 'belly' to make a bit of lard and therefore a few scratchings, for the lucky person who was having it.

Nell, a widow, living in Thriftwicket Lane, often had several 'bellies' a year from different farms. On one occasion, Nell was to have the belly from the Mansion House pig. She arrived in good time before the killing had taken place, and was encouraged to have a glass or two of good rumpunch cider while she waited for her prize. With a sackcloth apron tied tightly around her waist, Nell gathered up the two hanging corners, the belly was placed in the apron, and Nell was on her way home. The belly was easy to clean if it was done before the fat congealed. Struggling up Steppy Lane, the effects of the cider began to tell on Nell. She sat down for a rest, then lay down and slept. Her grip on the corner of her apron relaxed and the belly slithered out to lie all over Nell. Meanwhile, Bumble, who lived at Bank House, Thriftwicket Lane, was on his way down to the Mansion House for a plate of 'pig's fry' that had been promised. Misreading the situation, thinking that the poor old girl's stomach had burst, it was claimed that you could hear his cries for help a mile away.

The Travelling Cider Mill

The mobile cider mill which travelled around the farms of the parish and its neighbours was run and owned by 'Cider Billy', William Norgrove of Chapel Farm, Hayton Bent. My father, Andrew Smout, was mill assistant and chief taster to the said Cider Billy. They travelled for many miles with the mill loaded onto a horse drawn dray, their bikes tied on top so that they were able to cycle back home in the evenings from distant farms. A great deal of cider was made in those days; no farm was said to be complete without its cider and perry. Many farmers saw the supplying of cider or perry to be part of the wages, but the husband's or father's gut being full of free cider and perry, paid as part of a wage, meant that his family would not benefit.

Huge quantities of cider and perry were made until the Second World War, but with the coming of tractors and motorized machinery, the drinking of cider more or less ended. This was because the workers needed a clear head to operate such machinery; the farmer therefore refused to supply cider, partly because of the cost of such machinery, and partly because of safety considerations. Orchards were grubbed up, and turned into grass or corn land.

Electricity

The people living in Stanton Lacy village and those at Lower and Upper Hayton were able to have electricity put in some nine years before the rest of the parish. The Ludlow Peaton line had been erected in 1940 to supply the Peaton factories with power. After the war many people paid to have the power put into their homes, but only those properties close to the line were considered. It was not until 1956 that the people of Hayton Bent and the surrounding area were able to have electric power.

Piped Water

In 1962-63, the piped water supply was put in by the forerunners of the Severn Trent. Not all people in the parish had it laid on and even now a few families are still on their own private supply. Before 1963, supplies had been obtained from private wells or community wells, open, or fitted with pumps with which to hand pump the water to the surface. These wells would often run dry in a hot summer, when one was forced to walk to the nearest public well to obtain a bucket of drinking water.

Stock was also driven long distances to water. One old gent who owned a house cow had to make a round trip of $1\frac{1}{2}$ miles to take his cow to water every evening. He also took two buckets with him in which to carry drinking water for the house. I quote:

> I did take the owd cow down to drink, and I taked me buckets oth I to bring some for the 'ouse, when I got the own bugger there, 'er 'udna drink. I waited a bit, then I thought bugger ya. I filled me buckets an' started for whoam, driving the owd cow. When I reached the top of the 'ill an' was in sight of the 'ouse, I sits on the edge bank an' lit me pipe, damn me, when I was busy lighting the pipe, the owd cow drunk both buckets of water, an' I 'as to walk down there agen.

The coming of the piped supply was a godsend in some ways, but the unpalatable water that runs from the taps smelling strongly of chemicals, cannot be any asset to one's health despite what we are brainwashed into believing by the powers that be!

☆ ☆ ☆ ☆

Local run services had also existed for there had been butchers shops at North Cottage and the Mine House, blacksmiths at Hayton Bent and Stanton Lacy. High Croft was a shop selling most things up until the 1940s, and there had been such shops at Stanton Lacy and Lower Hayton. Dixon Place had sold a selection of household needs. High Grove had sold confectionery from its post office, Browns Corner had also carried on this trade when it became the post office in the 1950s. There had been a tailor's shop at Quarry Cottage, a Patch house on the Bullring, a clock and watch repairer on Titterhill Road. Ernest Wilde was the local barber, living at Hopton Gate. Mrs. Went, the blacksmith's wife, sold tobacco and confectionery from the Smithy house. The Rowe and Evison families carried out the trade of carpenter, wheelwright and coffin makers to the parish.

The Smith and Lock families, working out of their travelling caravans, sold all manner of cottons, silks, buttons, elastic and clothes pegs, these the women folk hawked around in huge baskets, walking out from Ludlow or Craven Arms when hey based their homes there in the winter months, spending the nights in barns throughout their lengthy rounds.

The Stephens family did the rounds in their donkey drawn flat bottomed carts, collecting rabbit skins, rags, bottles and many other things. They paid the farmers with rock salt for any goods they had from them. The Marsh family of Ludlow also ran a similar service, but paid in cash.

All these services and activities ceased at the end of World War II. Automation killed off the need for local services, the older people who could not, or would not ever drive their own transport, were not even considered. This trend still exists in all country areas, there being very little thought given to the elderly. We shall of course, all grow old—if we live long enough!

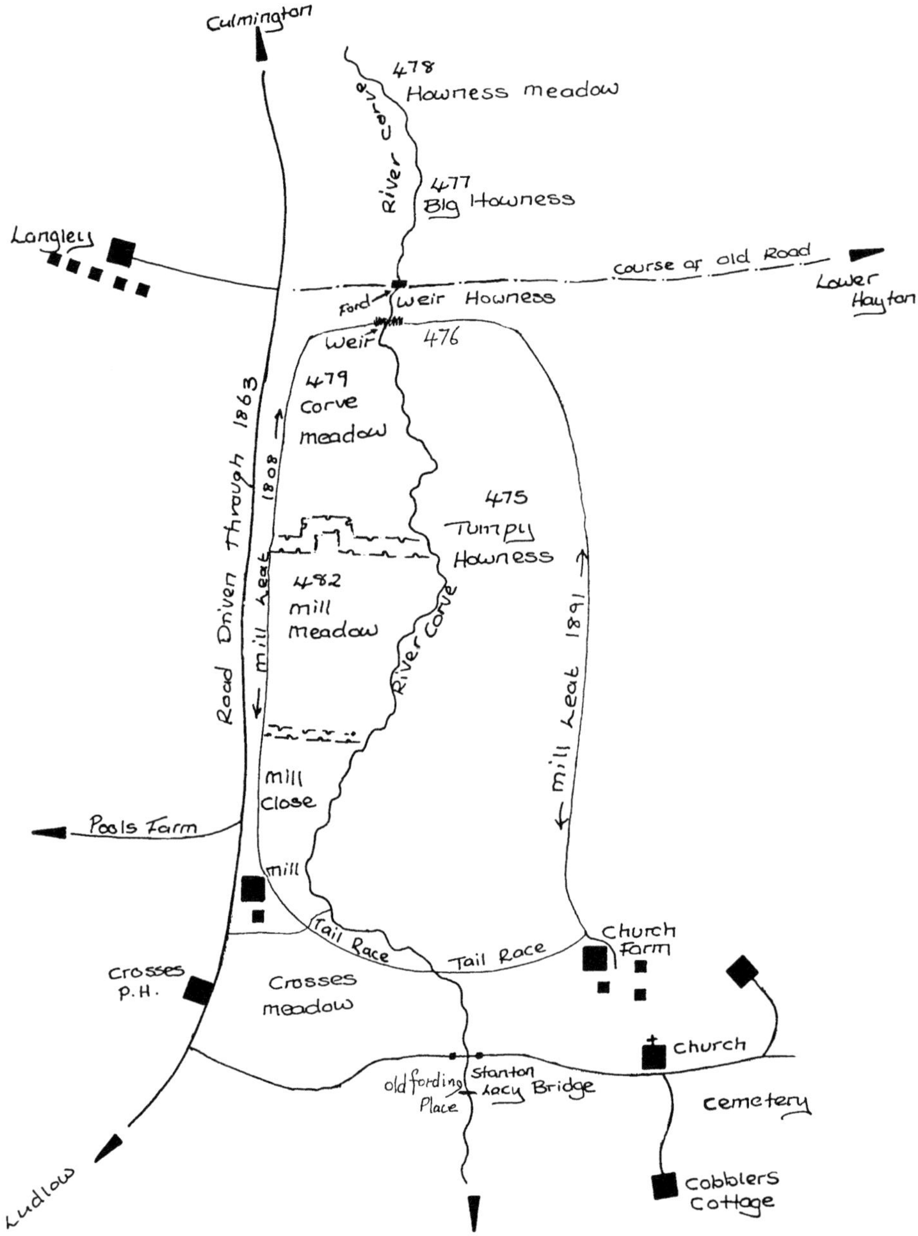

Map of Stanton Lacy's watermills

CHAPTER XXIII

Water Mills of Stanton Lacy Parish

Records of the corn mills of Stanton Lacy are few, but with much research, it has been possible to trace six of them!

Stanton Lacy Mill

The first mill in the village of Stanton Lacy was situated at SO 492792 and part was still standing well into the 1950s. To pick up the mill leat, we must travel up the B4365 to Langley. On the right hand side of the road, and on the east side of the River Corve, there existed until the 1960s several fields, all with a similar name: Howness Meadow, Big Howness, Tumpy Howness, and Weir Howness. None of these fields can now be identified as all the hedges have been removed. Howness derives from the Old English for anything that was similar.

It is parcel 476, Weir Howness, in which we are interested, for remains of the weir can still be seen on the River Corve. From the weir the water flowed along the leat which ran for approximately 1,100 yards down to Stanton Lacy Mill. The mill itself was situated in parcel 482, Mill Meadow. The B4365 follows closely the line of the redundant leat and indeed is built over it in some places. It is possible that the leat was made redundant when the Bridgnorth, Much Wenlock, Ludlow road was put through in 1863. Baugh's survey map of 1808 gives the mill a symbol, suggesting that it was still a working mill in 1808.

By the 1930s the mill had been stripped down to walls that stood only 4 ft. high on top of which a wooden building had been built in tongue and groove boards, roofed in corrugated iron. This made a good strong building out of the redundant mill and Shropshire County Council Highways Department used it for storage up until the 1950s.

One may think that it was nothing short of vandalism to knock down the mill, which at the time it ceased operation would still have been a stout durable building. The simple truth is that as the mills were being built, the heavy machinery was installed and the walls built around it, so it was necessary to dismantle the building to remove the valuable machinery when the mill ceased to be operational.

The Tithe Map of 1847-49, shows the mill leat on the west side of the river, agreeing with Baugh, but does not show a mill symbol.

All later maps from 1847-49, show the watercourse on the east side of the river, terminating at SO 495789, Stanton Cottage Farm, proving that the mill was moved to this location after 1847-49, probably at the time the now B4365 road was put through in 1863. There remains evidence at Church Farm that the mill was moved to this location, but ceased to be a water driven mill around 1890, turning to steam power around this time. I hasten to add that this statement was picked up from local people. I do not have any written record of a steam driven mill!

In 1850 the mill owner is recorded as the Earl of Craven, and the miller as Herbert Blakeway.

Wootton Mill

The hamlet of Wootton formed part of Stanton Lacy Parish until 1879, and a mill had been in use here for hundreds of years. A new mill was built in the late part of the 18th century to replace the old one, but there are records that both mills were operational at the same time for a number of years. A mill leat of some 1,200 yards which took the water from the River Onny was named the 'roaring bolt' probably said with tongue in cheek considering the sluggishness of the Onny. The records of 1840 show the owner of Wootton Mills to be the Earl of Craven and the miller, Roger Blakeway.

Hope Mill

Very little evidence of the mill (OS 512787) remains, just the base of the building and some evidence of a leat. There is rumoured to have been a thriving mill here up until the early 19th century, but I have no records.

Lower Hayton Mill

The exact location of this mill cannot be traced, but possible sites are few and far between! However, from the records we can be sure that a water mill existed here in 1280, belonging to the Devereux family.

Upper Hayton Mill

This mill stood on Witchcot brook (OS 522811). Unlike the two previous mills, the exact location of this mill is known. The base of the mill was still standing in the 1940s, though very little evidence can now be found for, like other mills, the building was demolished to remove the machinery. Stones from the building have gone to sites elsewhere and all that now remains is one large stone that has had a hole drilled through it, and must have been some type of anchoring stone, and a few stones along the brook that turned the water to the mill. The two mill stones are now at the White House, Lower Hayton, where they have been taken for safe keeping by the owner.

Wheat terraces in the fields around the mill are still in evidence, many others having now been ploughed out, but it is possible to get an idea why this mill was located in such a remote spot. The roadway to and from the mill ran over the shoulder of the hill, then over the Common to Hayton Bank.

Jerry Morgan, cowkeeper of The Yew Tree, The Bullring, worked in Hayton Mill. Jerry was a real cadger of other people's tobacco and would try to cadge a pipeful off any visitor to or worker at the mill. Smoking a short clay pipe that would only hold a thimblefull of tobacco, Jerry looked harmless enough to those who were not in the know, but once the unsuspecting had handed over their pouch, a huge cherrywood pipe was produced from Jerry's inside pocket. This pipe was said to hold at least enough to fill 10 clays. Jerry would ram it in far too tightly, and then make a great show of trying to light it, until the victim had turned away, and left the mill. Jerry would then fill his 'clay' from the cherry time and time again.

Needless to say, this could not be seen to continue by some of the younger victims of Jerry's greed, and a plot was hatched! A casual visitor arrived at the mill carrying an ample supply of Biggs Red Bell Tobacco. He had a few words with the miller while he filled and lit his pipe.

'Could'st spare I a pipeful Gaffer?' Inquired Jerry.

'Certainly!' Came the answer. True to form Jerry produced his huge cherry. 'You carry on with what you are doing,' said the visitor, 'I will fill it for you.' But tobacco was not all that our visitor was carrying, and filling

Jerry's cherry two thirds full of Red Bell he then placed a layer of Black Gun Powder on top of this, topping off with more Red Bell firmly rammed. Jerry returned for his pipe, the visitor produced matches and insisted that Jerry light up. To save face, Jerry got the pipe going with some difficulty, due to the top layer of tobacco being rammed too tightly—but he succeeded. Seconds later the pipe exploded burning Jerry's whiskers and hair, with minor injuries to his skin and lips. There is no doubt that this was a stupid act, and could have caused serious injury, but it is said that this incident went a long way to curing Jerry's cadging habit; he never replaced the cherry, and only begged a clay full if he was allowed to fill it himself. Jerry died at Yew Tree Cottage in the 1920s; an old man! It appears that he was far too tough to succumb to strong 'baccy', with or without gunpowder.

Lydehold Mill

There was a mill in the area of the Lydehole, but I am unable to discover any record of this building. Mill Cottage was built in 1835 and from this one would expect to find some trace of the mill which would have stood nearby. Maybe the cottage is part of thc old mill.

The 'Lydehole' close to Mill Cottage was used in the process of whitening flax and hemp. Perhaps these were spun into materials close by. Any type of industry where water was used was termed 'mill' by our ancestors, as this was a way of identifying places rather than trying to make something out to be grander than it was. Alternatively, a horse gin could have formed Lydehold Mill, or even a ropewalk. Horse gins were often used in rope making. The horse moved round in a small circle attached to a winding drum called a gin, new rope being spun from hemp by the mill was wound into coils this way, but more often, a rope walk was in use. In this a boy would hold the new rope over his shoulder and walk slowly over a certain distance, keeping the rope taut as it was slowly spun and twisted by the spinning reel. This practice was said to have been terribly hard on the small boy's hands, the new ropes often snagging on the spinner and burning the rope walker's hands. Our ancestors were not too fussy when referring to such places as mills.

But having said this, I am not happy. The Lydehole and the adjoining hamlet of Sutton Hill consisted of 15 dwellings up until the end of the 1940s, they could not have survived without a corn mill from when the hamlet was first formed around 1725. A building demolished in the 1940s stood on the south side of Lydehole brook, approximately 100 metres from Mulberry Lane.

This may have been the mill, the miller living away from the mill in the cottage known as Mill Cottage, though this would have meant him living in the adjoining parish of Diddlebury as the brook here forms the parish boundary.

CHAPTER XXIV

Parish Ghosts

There are four areas of Stanton Lacy that are supposed to be haunted, generations of parishioners having claimed to have witnessed the sightings of the supernatural.

The Gurly Hole Ghost

One such place is the Gurly Hole, the old disused quarry that is situated at OS 497786 off Carpenters Lane, near to the rear entrance to Manor Farm, where there have been many sightings of a young woman dancing round the quarry's rim at full moon. Rumours were that a woman had committed suicide here in the 19th century, but how she had taken her life never became clear to me. A jump from the top of the quarry would hardly be sufficient to bring about a fatality. Perhaps she secreted herself in the quarry and killed herself by some other means. Whatever the answer, many people claim to have seen this ghost.

When we were young lads, having left school, got jobs and managed to afford a bike, we met at Stanton Lacy in the lighter evenings to play football and cricket, swim in the Corve or do many other things. We would go to the Gurly Hole when the moon was full yet when we considered it dark enough for the ghost to make an appearance. I never saw anything on my visits, but some of the members of the gang would be rooted to the spot with fear, claiming that they could see her. I have wondered many times if such things do exist: do they only reveal themselves to those who do believe, or do people of a nervous disposition imagine that they see these apparitions, a figment of their own imaginations? There are many who would try to tell me that these ghosts do exist, but without proof, it would be a waste of their and my time!

The Church Ghost

There have been reports of some people having feelings of not being alone, and being aware of 'something evil' on entering St. Peters Church. Dogs have turned tail and bolted out of the door, to crouch trembling in fear in the churchyard. On the few occasions that I have entered the church, I have experienced no such feelings, even taking my two Scottish Border Collies with me to prove a point on several visits. But as I have said, if the supernatural does exist, perhaps they only reveal themselves to those that believe in them.

I have known lads who were living in the cottages on Ludlow Racecourse or in the village of Bromfield, who have cycled home through Ludlow and up the A49 to reach home rather than cycle down Carpenters Lane or Blacksmiths, where they would have to pass the churchyard, so great was their fear after a night's 'Ghost Spotting' as we called it.

Hopton Gate Ghost

If the subject of ghosts was ever brought up in his company, dad always remained quiet. It appeared that he had on several occassions seen, or thought he had seen, something that was beyond his comprehension. But when we were young he never revealed these sightings to us kids, saying: 'Them that is jud conna 'urt ya bwoy; its them buggers that's living ya wonts to kep yer eye on!'

One night during the blackout of World War II, Dad arrived home pale and somewhat disturbed. 'I have sin the bugger, mother!' He informed Mum. 'Crossed the road in front of me, just as I was approaching the Smithy.' Mother dismissed the idea that he had seen the Hopton Gate Ghost, putting his sighting down to the over indulgence in rumpunch cider—but he was sober. Dad was not a person who was easily scared; he had seen active service on the Somme and in Flanders, horrors that were not the figments of an imagination.

The Hopton Ghost appeared as man and dog with an aura of blue light surrounding both, so they were plainly seen. Many of the older folk of the area had claimed to have witnessed the ghost crossing the road, and always at the same spot. The hedges on both sides of the road at this point were overgrown and neglected, so it would have been impossible for anyone who may have been having a joke to have walked through them.

Father lived for 28 years after his sighting, but never walked there again during the hours of darkness.

The Ghost of Charlie Smout

Charles Edward Smout was born around 1826-27, at Sutton Hill in the parish of Diddlebury. When he was nineteen years old, Charlie, as he was known, walked from his home to London with the sole intention of joining the army. Being a fine figure of a man, Charlie joined the 11th Hussars, rose to sergeant, and was said to have enjoyed army life. In the mid-1850s Charlie was posted to the Crimea, where he served with the Light Brigade under James Thomas Brudenell, 7th Earl of Cardigan, at the Battle of Balaclava.

The Heavy Brigade had had great success on the field and Cardigan was itching to show what his Light Brigade was made of. His desires brought about one of the biggest disasters ever for the British Army. The Light Brigade, armed with just lances and sabres, were ordered to charge the Russian and Cossak artillery which were positioned in a valley later known as the Valley of Death. The result of this charge was the destruction of the Light Brigade, with the death of most of its Lancers and Hussars. 'The Charge of the Light Brigade' was immortalized by Tennyson's poem, some 30 years after it had taken place.

Charlie was one of the luckier ones, just having his left leg shattered beyond repair and which was amputated above the knee in a field hospital on the battlefield. Charlie was invalided out of the army with a pension of around 7/8d per week, (roughly 37p), and returned to his parents' home, they having now moved to The Bullring, Hayton Bent.

Charlie was a broken man, the wound did not heal properly and was aggravated by a poorly fitting 'peg leg'. Charlie took to drinking any strong liquor that he could buy or beg; this, when taken in large quantities, helped to deaden the pain. But things went from bad to worse; Charlie roamed the lanes anytime during day or night cursing Lord Cardigan, Florence Nightingale, Tsar Nicholas I, and anyone else he considered might be responsible for his present condition. He would, no doubt, have also cursed Tennyson if the poem immortalizing the disaster had been written at that time.

Things got out of hand. Some of the young men tried to take a raise out of Charlie when he was drunk, and several had their heads cracked by Charlie's crutch, which it is said he could wield much as he had wielded a sabre in his army days. Complaints were made and investigated, and the authorities decided that he would be 'taken in'. This meant a period of time in the Asylum, as there were no mental hospitals for the likes of him in those days.

Here I will quote great great grandmother's account as handed down through the generations:

> They said they would fetch him on the Thursday. Charlie said he would never go, but on the Thursday morning got up, shaved, washed, waxed his moustache, dressed in his suit and boot(!), had a bit of breakfast, he seemed quiet and sobre. About half an hour before noon, he went outside. (The officials from Shrewsbury were expected to arrive about midday). About that time I heard footsteps on the yard. 'Where is he?' Demanded Mr. Lee the local overseer who was in company with the men from Salop. (Lee Edwards was the overseer, but was referred to as Mr. Lee—his father still living at this time.)
>
> 'He's about outside.' I said. One of the gents searched the cottage, Mr. Lee and the other searched outside. There was no sign of Charlie. 'He might be down by the watering stile,' I said, 'he often sits down there!'
>
> 'Show us!' They demanded.
>
> As we passed the drovers spring, I cried 'No! Charlie, no!' I could see his leg and peg, swinging from the old ash tree by the stile. I tried to hold him up to take the weight off his neck.
>
> 'He's dead.' One of the gents said, 'Let him hang there until the Constable can be informed, he must attend to keep things legal.'

Charlie's body was removed later that day, and taken away from this area. An order to take Charlie in to the Asylum had come into force from midday, so now he was their responsibility.

Charlie's ghost was first seen some 12 months after his suicide, when many local people claimed to have seen it swinging along the lanes in the area with the gait of a one-legged man. We were made aware of the story of Charlie's ghost at a young age, when older children went to the spot to frighten themselves, and returned claiming to have witnessed all manner of things. Many of my family claimed to have seen the family ghost; Dad had seen it but did not talk about his sighting until many years had passed.

I, who do not believe in Heaven, Hell, God, the Devil, Ghosts, or anything remotely connected with religion, believe it to be something concocted to ease the thought of the end by those who have great fear of dying. I consider it all a fairy story, deserving a ranking somewhere between 'Goldilocks and the Three Bears' and 'Jack and the Beanstalk'!

But on the night of January 26th, 1958, I came close to having my thoughts on the supernatural completely turned around. Having served as a regular in the British Army, I was home on leave, after a tour of duty on the island of Cyprus, and I made my way back to the family home in Thriftwicket Lane. There being very little to do, and having no transport, I walked over to the Royal Oak at Culmington, our local pub having closed its doors for the last time the previous year.

The night of January 26th was very dark and foggy, and having reached the Wrens Nest stile situated on the public footpath from Lower Hayton on my return journey, I stopped to rest and have a smoke. I leaned on the top bar of the stile, supporting my weight on my forearms. The stile was made from willow rails, and had plenty of give in the top bar. Suddenly I became aware that I was not alone. Another person, or something that resembled a person in shape, was standing close to me, leaning forward on the stile as I was. There had been no movement of the bar, so the shape was weightless. The hair on my head stood up. 'Charlie!' I croaked. The Shape faded away before my eyes.

I must admit that this experience unsettled me somewhat; it being something that I did not understand. Returning to the stile at first light, my footprings were plain to see, but mine, and mine alone. There was no sign that anyone else had been there.

Mentioning my sighting to Dad, he said 'It was old Charlie. I met him close to there when I came back in 1919; he stood in front of me for a full minute. He was just welcoming us back home bwoy!'

I have returned to the Wrens Nest stile on many occassions, but I have never been aware of a presence since. Visits on the anniversary of Charlie's death (15th September), on the anniversary of my sighting (26th January), at the full of the moon—all have been in vain.

Since returning to live at Hayton, I have taken my two Scottish Border Collies with me, Collies being the most intelligent of all breeds, but they have never shown any sign of alarm. Despite my experience, I still do not believe in ghosts!!!

The Ghost of Witchcot Wood

The ghost of Witchcot Wood turned out to be nothing more sinister than the local gamekeeper, draped in a white sheet. The ghost ran about the ride at dusk, crying 'Woooh ooooh'. If it had kept quiet he may have scared us lads off, but with his breeches and leggings and high boots being plainly visible from under the sheet, he scared no one!

CHAPTER XXV

Public Houses of Stanton Lacy

Stanton Lacy although quite a large parish, has no pub, which all us normal people who like a drink and a chat in a relaxed atmosphere find most vexing!

Before the shrinking of the parish by a 'local Government Board Order' in 1879, when all its detached areas were transferred to other parishes, Stanton Lacy could boast that it had once had at least 14 pubs and cider houses.

It has not been possible to find records of the exact opening and closure dates of all the public houses of Stanton Lacy, as the parish records are not forthcoming. Some have been entered in the records as 'Public House', someas 'Inn', another as a 'Beer House' or 'Cider House'. The differences in terms are that a 'Public House' was a building holding a licence to sell alcoholic drinks; an 'Inn' was a public house which also served food and provided accommodation, a 'Beer House' was licenced to sell beer only, and supply and sell bread and cheese, whilst a 'Cider House' wa s allowed to sell cider only, and also supply and sell bread and cheese.

New Inn Hayton: This was the last parish pub to close. Being specially built as a pub and opening in 1820, the New Inn was finally closed on 11th February 1957.

Cross Keys, Corve Bridge, Ludlow: The Cross Keys closed in 1917 when it was within the confines of Ludlow, and was later demolished to allow for alterations to the Shrewsbury to Hereford railway line.

Nelson, Rock Green: Still open, but now in the confines of Ludow.

Dun Cow, Rock Green: Closed around 1880 when no longer in the parish, now a farmhouse.

New Inn, Rock Green: Still in the parish when closed; demolished around 1860.

Raven Inn, East Hamlet: Still open but now within the confines of Ludlow.

Greyhound Inn, Upper Galdeford: Not in the parish since 1879, The Greyhound closed in 1937, and was demolished for redevelopment of the area in the 1970s.

Mitre House, Corve Bridge, Ludlow: The Mitre House closed in 1871, when still within the Parish of Stanton Lacy. It is now an antique shop.

New Inn, New Road, Ludow: The New Inn closed in the 1880s, but had been placed in the confines of Ludlow in 1879.

Crosses Inn, Stanton Lacy: The Crosses Inn closed between 1851 and 1861, it has not been possible to find the actual year of its closure

Craven Arms, Stanton Lacy: The Craven Arms closed around the 1870s, shortly after the Earls of Craven had sold the village.

Halfway House, Ludlow Peaton Road: The Halfway House closed around 1830, it has not been possible to find the actual date. It probably served cider only, forming a link in the chain of public or cider houses situated along the drovers' roads.

Hopes Public House, Upper Hayton: The Hopes Public House closed during the 1840s or '50s. It was still open during the survey of 1841, where it is entered as 'Beerhouse', with beerhouse keeper Samuel Weaver. The survey of 1861 makes no mention.

The Patch House, The Bullring, Upper Hayton: The Patch House, known locally as The Pound and Patch, closed around 1820, but was from then on a private dwelling until the early part of this century. The remains of the building were demolished in the 1970s. It is considered that only cider was served here. Many cider houses were situated along the drovers' roads with their pounds in which the driven animals were enclosed at night.

CHAPTER XXVI

Hayton Platoon Home Guard

The Home Guard operated from Downton Hall, Walter Bailey, Head Gamekeeper for Downton Hall Estates, being commanding officer of the platoon. He, together with Sgt. Major Tipton and Sgt. William Henner of No.2 Hayton Bent, kept this platoon going for the duration of the war, or at least until the threat of invasion had passed.

Many of the old soldiers who had returned from the battlefields of the 1914-18 war refused to join the Home Guard, including my father who just simply refused to ever bow his head, or bend his knee to anyone after the disasters of the First World War. He also felt that our high command had drunk and whored its way around Paris, while the men died in their thousands through lack of correct leadership or purpose. Father returned home from the Somme and Flanders firmly believing that the term 'Sir' was just another name for a 'Bloody Fool'.

Despite some or most of the old sweats who had seen the horrors of battle refusing to serve, Hayton Platoon was always up to strength. The playground at Hayton School served as parade ground in the summer. From here they marched off to Cuckoo Pen Coppice, or down to Tanners Barn to the range. Cuckoo Pen Coppice was used for mock battles or fieldcraft and Whitbatch range for rifle practice, where the targets were set at the foot of the hill to the left of Whitbatch Farm looking from Tanners Barn.

At the beginning of the war, the older boys from the school at Hayton had been called in to help the Home Guard in their preparations for repelling an invasion. Tree limbs, some 12 ft. high, were dug upright into any field considered to be a possible landing place for aircraft or gliders, the theory being that anything that tried to land would be smashed to pieces, or that these upright posts would deter anything from trying to land in the first place.

Tank traps were set up at the Hayton Cross Roads, and at the top of the Hope. These consisted of steel bars and concrete blocks placed across the road and which were supposed to be capable of ripping the tracks off enemy tanks. The Home Guard assembled these traps at regular intervals and manned them for a few hours, then dismantled them and rolled them to the side of the road. I'm sure they knew that if enemy tanks approached, they would simply have driven through the roadside hedge, so avoiding the traps, without reducing speed. Still, the Home Guard had to be seen to be trying, thus encouraging others to try.

All the shotguns, except where it could be proved that there was a need for one, were commandeered for military use. These privately owned shotguns were traced through licence holders, so as father had never had a gun licence, he kept his. It was a valuable part of our survival kit as a family. Special cartridges were made for these shotguns. Some held just one single ball of lead as big as a marble—these were to kill German paratroopers. Others held five smaller balls of lead—these were to fire through the fuel tanks of invading vehicles. These balls of lead were effective enough for their intended purpose, but were not so good for the killing of rabbits, hares and pheasants. The reason was that one had to be more accurate, a difficult task on a moonlit night—but we survived!

The single ball cartridges for the destruction of human beings nearly passed their test one Saturday night in 1944. With the danger of an invasion long gone, a bus service to and from Ludlow had sprung up on a fairly regular basis. Greens Motors ran from Ludlow to Middleton, then up to Hopton Cangeford, Hopton Gate, Hayton Cross Roads, through to Clee St. Margaret. Here the bus turned around and retraced its journey back to Ludlow. The bus ran with hooded lights: people were still cautious! Ned, a firey member of the Home Guard was on duty at the Hopton Cangeford turn, with the instructions to stop all vehicles and find out the name of its driver and the destination of the vehicle. Bert, who was driving the returning empty coach, swore that he never saw Ned, which is why he failed to stop. Ned, however, claimed that Bert must have noticed him because the bus had struck him a glancing blow. Whatever the truth, Bert did not stop when he should have. Ned fired both barrels of his shotgun into the back of the retreating bus, bringing it to a shuddering stop a little way down the road. Both single lead balls had gone through the back of the bus and, it is said, had passed through the backs of four seats before being a spent force. Bert, the owner-driver of the bus, had to pay a huge fine at the following court case, whilst Ned was commended for his dedication to duty and orders! One can only wonder if Ned would have received the same commendation if the bus had been full of passengers.

CHAPTER XXVII

'Hayton Platoon' Army Cadet Force

'B' Platoon, Army Cadet Force, was formed in 1946. The summer headquarters were at Rose Cottage, The Bullring, where parades were called every Thursday evening during the spring, summer and autumn. Winter parades were held in the old school, not yet the Parish Hall! Our Platoon Commander lived at Rock Cottage, The Bullring, but also owned Rose Cottage, which had remained empty since my family had moved out in 1934.

The platoon was only a small one of 14 members. We drilled, held mock battles, read maps and performed other duties expected of good cadets. Our main aim was to be seen as young soldiers who were learning something that would give us an advantage when called up for National Service at the age of eighteen. We were all issued with uniforms that had been made for soldiers during the war, which needless to say were far too large for our boyish figures; the 'battle blouses' hung on our slim frames like shrouds, the trousers hung with the behinds virtually dragging on the ground. The berets, new and unused, were like dustbin lids! Our mothers did their best to get the clothing to fit, but it was a really hopeless task; however, with the baggy clothing gathered up and held together with a tight webbing belt, we managed. Father, with two of his mates from the 1914-18 war, came to see us on parade. All three agreed that we looked like 'fourteen bags filled with "shit" bound in the middle!' Despite these insults we soldiered on.

A .22 rifle range was set up at Titterhill Quarry, which was, and still is common Land. Ludlow Platoon, who had their headquarters at the Drill Hall, Portcullis Lane, Ludlow, sometimes came up to shoot against us or to take us on in a mock battle. On rare occasions, we were transported down to the Drill Hall in a one ton Ford truck. These visits one way or the other turned into real battles, ending up in blood and often tears from some of the more emotional members of the platoons. Fists freely flew, with the boot and rifle butt often going in, but it was all good fun—I don't think that anyone really bore any malice.

The .22 rifle, (we only had one—our normal arms being short Lee Enfields 303s with blanks), had many uses. Having gained a marksman's badge with the .22, I was often called upon by the platoon commander to poach for him. Being a Brummie he often returned to Birmingham for weekends and liked to take the spoils of the countryside with him. Meat still being rationed, I shot rabbits and hares which were abundant at this time. My victims were often great distances away in shooting terms and I left them where they fell, collecting them when I was sure the coast was clear, receiving 6d (2½p) for each item. We know that these activities were against the law, but I did not really feel any concern, and being encouraged by an 'officer' and therefore a 'gentleman', what could I do?

Winter parades called at the old school were often non-starters, as our platoon commander had a drink problem and was often too drunk to walk from The Bullring up to the school. On those occasions when he did not put in an appearance, we made use of the available sports kit—a football, a 14lb medicine ball and two pairs of boxing gloves. With all three sports taking place at the same time, all hell broke loose!

In 1948, 'B' Platoon's life suddenly ended, not due to any fault of the squaddies, but due to our commander who, being fed up with carrying drinking water from Collects Well in the field by the Victorian Methodist Chapel, decided to bore and sink a well in the garden of Rock Cottage. Four of us cadets were commandeered to help. We dug down about 5 ft before hitting solid rock and, it being impossible to dig any deeper, were instructed to leave things be for the time being. A few days later we were summoned once again to Rock Cottage. This time we found the Captain from Ludlow Platoon present with our Lieutenant, and they had brought explosives to blow the rock at the bottom of the intended well. We bored a hole in the rock with a hand drill: tap and turn, tap and turn, a long drawn out operation. The charge was put into place, the whole lot attached to the plunger, which was situated on the yard of Rose Cottage, and the Captain set it off. The result was a mere barrow load of debris from the intended well, whilst shock waves shook the cottages as they travelled through the rock, breaking the windows of Rock, Rose, and Stone Cottages.

The Lieutenant owned both Rock and Rose Cottages, but the owner of Stone Cottage sued for damages. The officers, meanwhile, were reported to the police. As everyone thought, it turned out that the explosives had been taken without permission from an ammunition store in the Shrewsbury area. Hefty fines were imposed on both Captain and Lieutenant, and both lost their positions in the Cadet Corps. It was the end of 'B' Platoon. The Ludlow 'A' Platoon soon found a new platoon commander and carried on, but no adult was willing to take us on, perhaps one cannot blame them for their reluctance to do so!

CHAPTER XXVIII

Parish Flora & Fauna

The parish uplands consist of many small fields where flora and fauna still abound, unlike the valley bottoms where the hedges have been removed to make larger fields. With the removal of these hedges, together with the filling in of ponds, pools and waterways, much of the flora and fauna have been destroyed, but we can all hope that nature will triumph over greed in the end.

This loss of habitat has caused the common frog, toad and newt to be placed on the protected species list, whilst moorhen, curlew and lapwing are now rare in the area.

In the higher parts of the parish, many of the old rare plants still flourish. There can be found six species of orchid, the two species of twayblade, red and green heliborine, lady's mantle, lousewort, toothwort, broomrape, winter-green, bog myrtle, wild thyme, spurge laurel, wild gypsophilia and spring snowflake, even though, according to the experts, these last two species do not occur within this area!

Many of the hedgerows support the dormouse, and a nestbox scheme has been set up to monitor the population of this rare mammal.

Polecat and Roe deer are in evidence, whilst badger, fox, stoat, weasel, and grey squirrel are plentiful. The brown hare is becoming scarce; night lamping with dogs or rifles is the main reason for their decline. However, one is now more likely to encounter a hare in woodland than in open fields and this change in habitat will save them from extinction.

The rabbit lives on in pockets, for they too have changed their habits, probably unnoticed by man in the main. By living in small pockets, with a good distance between each of these populations, disease does not spread so

E.S.A. protected meadows, Hayton. The hedges are home to a colony of the rare dormouse

far so fast. Myxomatosis now wipes out an entire pocket, whereas the neighbouring pocket is untouched. It is my personal thought that man will never defeat this most persecuted of all animals.

Red kite and raven are to be seen, both having returned by courtesy of Aldon tip, where both species can be found scavanging. With the closing of this site imminent, we may once again lose both species.

Wild flower meadows

Meadows and hedges protected by E.S.A. grants, Upper Hayton

The buzzard, hobby, and goshawk are now nesting in the area, as are the tawny owl and little owl, with the re-introduction of the long-eared owl and the barn owl, things look promising for the owl populations. A rough legged buzzard was recorded feeding at Lower Hayton in the autumn of 1996. This of course, is just a one off, the species being a winter visitor in passing, but nevertheless, it is worth recording.

All in all the future of parish flora and fauna looks more promising than it has. With the parish uplands now an E.S.A., it is hoped things may improve—if the powers that be can get their act right. For any plant, bird, mamal or insect listed in Schedule 1 of The Wildlife and Countryside Act, a licence must be obtained from English Nature before any alteration can be made to its habitat, even if you're the owner of the land. But at the time of writing, this protection is not as complete as it seems, as grants are still being paid towards work which damages these species chances of survival. No one is suggesting that these acts are being carried out deliberately but, nevertheless, it is happening. We can only hope that M.A.F.F. will take advice from the organisations that are expert in these fields, such as The Botanical Society of the British Isles, The British Mammal Association, The Royal Society for the Protection of Birds and the various wildlife trusts.

Grants are a must. Farmers and Landowners must be rewarded in full for any inconvenience caused in, on, or around their properties. Then and only then shall we be successful in protecting what little flora and fauna we have left.

Huge fields with tramlines through them, the margins or headlands of the same fields yellowed and bare from chemical spraying, woodlands sprayed, killing off all unwanted growth, roadside margins sprayed—everything sprayed, and so killing off insects that form the basis of the food chain, bringing about a silent countryside, without life, excepting farm animals and humans! Is this the heritage we intend to leave for future generations?

Select Bibliography

Anglo Saxon Chronicles (1051)

Bagshaws' *Directory of Shropshire* (1851)

Baugh, Robert, Map of Shropshire (1808)

Beresford, *Deserted Villages of Shropshire* (1971)

Birmingham Enterprise Club Transactions

Board of Ordnance Map (1811)

Domesday Book

Hearth Tax Rolls

Lay Subsidy Rolls (1327)

Murchison, *Geology of Shropshire* (1839)

Parish Registers

Register of Public Houses

Rocque, John, Map of Shropshire (1752)

Shropshire Place Names

Tithe Commissioners Map (1848)

Turner, John, Map of Shropshire (1754)